overcoming toxic relationships

Creating Power from Past Pain

ALSO BY KELLEY (Kelly) R. PORTER

Perfectly Planned (Overcoming Incest, Rape & Sexual Abuse)

Perfectly Planned Workbook and Audiobook

Mental MakeOver (Creating a Positive Mindset) Book of Quotes

It's All About Life (Book of Poems)

Detox or DIEt
(Closing the Gap Between Death & Dis-Ease)

Copyrights © MMXIV by Kelley Porter

All rights reserved. Printed in the United States of America. No part of this book may be used or reproduced in any manner whatsoever without written permission except in the case of brief quotation embodied in critical articles and reviews. Nonfiction. Names and locations have been changed for the protection of privacy.

Cover Design by Julie Holloway
ISBN: 978-0-9851767-2-3

overcoming toxic relationships

A Non-Fiction Novel
By

KELLEY R PORTER, CERTIFIED LIFE COACH

Dedication

This book is dedicated to the men and women of the world who seek understanding of a toxic relationship versus a nontoxic. Those who were wounded as a child or as an adult. Those who are on a self-seeking journey and ready to improve their lives as a whole. Those who want to have successful relationships. Those who are willing to self-reflect and correct behaviors and patterns that hinder them from living a healthy lifestyle. Those who are ready to live in their truth and walk in forgiveness.

I can assure you this road can be accomplished if you are willing to look deep within, admit to your emotional instabilities and focus on changing yourself instead of others.

Table of Contents

1. Another Woman's Man — 1
2. Cheating Bisexual — 21
3. Mama's Boy — 45
4. Love Child — 73
5. Karma — 81
6. Inability to Walk — 96
7. Cutting Ties — 108
8. Taking My Power Back — 122
9. The Power of Self-Love — 138
10. Spiritual Journey — 194
11. Self-Reflection — 199
12. Trusting After Betrayal — 202
13. Forgiveness — 204
14. Have No Fear — 206

Foreword

Most of us know when it comes to giving up personal space it is the toughest thing one has to do. Not only are you sharing your life, you are also learning to conform to someone else's, and becoming one is not as easy as you may think. Sometimes in these situations the toxicity level becomes so incredibly high, one of you are bound to have a clash and some will become irreversible.

Kelley has shed light and her experiences with you in hopes of your relationship learning the steps to make you stick together like glue. Enjoy!

Rick Party, Radio Personality
HOT105
Miami, Florida

Prologue

After twenty years of abuse that included, incest, sexual, physical and verbal abuse, being drugged and raped, abandoned by my mother and forgiving my abusers, I still had a long way to go. The fact that I was basically born into abuse, I never really had the opportunity to grow and mature into the real me. I was mostly a product of abuse who survived. I didn't realize this was only the beginning of where I was headed and who I am today. A product of lies, deception and betrayal I grew quite fond of. At twenty eight years old, I started over trying to identify myself. The next ten years were filled with toxic relationships, abuse, self-betrayal, patterns and behaviors I developed after being abused as a child. I had no idea the life I was born into set the tone for me to accept ten more years of what only I could save myself.

Those two decades of abuse were a real challenge to my mind, body and soul. I forgave my abusers and moved forward, but moved forward into what? A young woman destined for more pain. Destined to be disrespected, mistreated and served another plate of hell. But this time, I had no one to blame but myself.

I was confused about what love was and had no idea of exactly who I was. On another path of destruction, these next ten years would make, or break me. In fact, thirty years of abuse, toxic relationships, and uncertainties would demolish anyone, but sit back, relax and watch the power unfold from pain.

This is my story and unfortunately a reality for many.

Another Woman's Man - 1

June 1999
"Are you Kelley?"
"Yes. I am. Why?"
"I'm Grace, Daniel's woman. Are you sleeping with him?"
"No, I am not."
"He told me you all slept together."
"He lied to you."
"We've been together for eleven years and I'd appreciate it if you would just step back."
"We are only friends."
"Okay."

We both walked out of the locker room. At this particular time, Daniel and I had known each other for about a week and although I told Grace we hadn't slept together, indeed we did. I never agreed with a woman approaching another woman about a man. Maybe if they married, but, the way Grace approached me, was very tasteful and respectful.
"Where did he go?"
"He probably ran."
I stood there looking around and Grace left. About five minutes later, Daniel appeared.
"Where did you go? Why did you run?"
"I didn't want to talk to her. She's always starting sh*t."
"Did you know she was coming here?"
"Yea."
"Why did you invite me here with you?"
"Cus I don't give a f*ck."

Grace was Daniel's live in woman when I met him, and she was dark-skinned, medium build, short hair and about five feet, seven inches tall. Her demeanor appeared very nice and respectful, but I found out later the person that confronted me in the Bally's locker room was all a façade. Daniel and I sat in his car for a while and talked. Some of the things he told me were more than enough reason for me to walk away. The fact that he had a woman was enough reason for me to not get involved in the first place.

"Why are you crying?"
"I hate this sh*t I'm going through. I got a woman pregnant, and I don't want any more kids. Grace has judged me since then."
"Why don't you ask her to leave?"
"I have, but she ain't left yet."
"If you really want her out, you will get her out. Stop crying and let's go."
Daniel and I drove over to Michael's Department store.
"Damn you're fine. What do you want with me?"
"You're fine too."
Daniel's phone rang.
"Yea, Kelley is my friend. I don't want to be bothered with your ass, and I want you out my f*cking house! B*tch f*ck you!"

Daniel hung the phone up, and I stared off into space. I couldn't hear what Grace said, but based on his responses, I figured it out. I felt like I had nothing to do with that conversation. The worst part is, I never even thought for one moment, if he talked to her like that, he would talk to me like that. More red flags and I still ignored them.
"Daniel please don't invite me to Bally's anymore if you know she's coming. I don't want to be bothered with that."
"That's fine."

We made it to my place and Daniel never even took a bath. He stayed for a while and then went home. I took a hot bath, made dinner and watched TV for the rest of the night. *He needs to put her out and then I can see him as much as I want. She doesn't look like sh*t anyway. I really don't give a damn how she feels. If she's worried about him seeing me, then she needs to do her job.* I thought.
My phone rang.
"Hello."
"Hey Kelley, What are you doing today?"
"I'm off work so I'm getting ready to go to the gym."
"Which one?
"Dan Ryan."
"Okay. I will meet you up there."
"Hey you."
I smiled at Daniel.
"Hey baby."
Daniel hugged me.

Why in the hell are all these niggas staring at me? Probably because I slept with several of them. Or maybe because they know Daniel has a woman. Oh well. I thought. Daniel and I proceeded to work chest and back and had a wonderful workout. I met his family later that day. Daniel taught me a lot about weight lifting and training my muscles. He was the first man I had sex with and without the thoughts of being molested. He was the first man I allowed myself to connect with on an emotional level. I opened my heart completely for Daniel, and would've done just about whatever he asked.

Daniel's body was nicely chiseled, and he was so sexy to me. His personality was outgoing and he had a very bright sense of humor. He always made me laugh when he wasn't making me cry. I overlooked and accepted many red flags.

While I worked for the University of Chicago hospital, I sought employment in my new field as a Medical Laboratory Technologist. Daniel visited me at work many times during my lunch hour, and more than often, I was lunch in the back seat of his car. He knew much of my past and never judged me. He was very generous and never had a problem buying me clothes, taking me out or whatever I wanted to do. I was very happy to meet his family and from the outside looking in, everybody seemed to be perfect.

"Hey Ma, this is Kelley."
"Hi Kelley."
"Hi."
"You can call me Ms. Harris."
"How about I call you Mama?"
"That would be fine if."

Daniel's mother never finished her sentence and in fact, she dropped her voice. I didn't pay much attention to it, but I should have. Ms. Harris was soft-spoken, light-skinned with light brown eyes. She wore her hair short, colored somewhat red, and on occasion, blonde. She was about five feet nine, very overweight and had an extremely large bottom. She appeared kind and trustworthy, but she was hiding who she really was and is.

"Daniel told me about some things you went through when you were a child. Are you over those things?"
"I sure am."
"How did you get over being molested?"
"Prayer and acceptance."
"That's good."
"I really care about your son. He's a good man."
"You think so?"
"Yea, I do."
"I don't think it was a good idea for him to start something with another woman until he closed the door on the other."

I really didn't know how to respond to that. I was just happy we were together.

"Kelley are you ready?"

"Yea, I am."

"It was nice meeting you Ms. Harris."

"You too."

"I will talk to you later Mama."

Daniel and I left and headed out for cocktails.

"Your mother is very nice."

"Thank you. That's the only mother I have and won't tolerate any woman disrespecting her."

"I was taught better than that."

"That's good because I couldn't be with you if you were out of line with my mother. Grace had the nerve to get an attitude when my mother came by my place and hung a picture of her on my wall so she took it down and put it in the closet."

"What size was it?"

"A poster size, but that doesn't matter. That's my damn Mama."

"Oh wow, I can understand why she would take it down. That's where you and she live. Why does your mother need a poster size photo in your place? How did she get in?"

"She has keys."

"Your mother has keys to your place?"

"Yea."

"I guess that's understandable. My mother has my extra set, but she doesn't use them unless she's invited."

"My mother can come over as much as she likes. So let's just get off the subject of my mother."

That's good he respects his mother and I can say they are very close. Some people say when a man respects his mother, he will respect his woman. But that picture on the wall was a bit much. I would've taken that sh*t off my wall too. I hope he ain't no damn Mama's boy. I thought.

Daniel's relationship with his mother appeared healthy. There was nothing Daniel wouldn't do for his mother and I appreciated that. Ms. Harris appeared kind and very supportive of her sons. I learned later everything appeared to perfect, but was all a cover up for the true toxicity and dysfunction in their family.

"Why don't you answer that?"
During the entire car ride Daniel's phone wouldn't stop ringing.
"I don't feel like arguing with her ass."
"Is that Grace?"
"Hell yea."
"Talk to her."
I really didn't want Daniel to talk to her. I wanted him to cuss her out like he always did. When Daniel treated Grace like garbage it made me feel good. I felt like I was the one for him.

"Yea Grace. B*tch I don't give a f*ck. You can get the f*ck out of my house and never be bothered with me again! Don't worry about what the f*ck I'm doing!"
Daniel hung the phone up.
"F*cking b*tch. I hate her ass."
"Calm down Daniel and don't let her ruin our night."
"You know what, you're right. I'm turning this damn phone off. F*ck her."

Daniel and I went to the Other Place and had a few cocktails. The Other Place was a stepper's lounge located on the seventy-fifth between State & Michigan. Daniel wasn't really into Steppers music. He was a Rock lover and a huge fan of Jimmy Hendricks. We sat at the bar, talked about Grace again, and danced a bit. I didn't realize the liquor would add to his anger. While getting ready to leave, Daniel argued with another gentleman and exploded.
"F*ck you stupid motherf*cker!"
"Nigga go head on with that sh*t."
"Nigga I will come over there and beat your ass!"

"Will you please stop Daniel? You're upset with Grace and you're taking it out on everyone else. Don't allow her to do this to you." "Man I don't give a f*ck."
"Just get in the car and let's go home."
Daniel got in the car and we went back to my place. Daniel spent a night with me, and in the morning he went home. Later that day he called me.
"Hello."
"Hey Kelley, this b*tch up in my house talking sh*t. She scratched my damn face up."
"Were y'all fighting?"
"She started swinging at me and…… B*tch f*ck you! Get the f*ck out my house!"
"Is she there?"
"Yea. She's upstairs."
"Why don't you call the police on her?"
"I'm on my way over there."
"Okay."

I hope he calls the police on her ass and have her locked up. Any woman who hits a man needs her ass knocked out. That's just dumb as hell. He will get tired and eventually beat her ass. I thought.

Daniel's relationship with Grace was completely disruptive and he was adamant about her leaving his house. They argued practically all the time and it appeared as if he hated her. Daniel always said he wasn't sleeping with her, but deep down inside, I knew he was. I really didn't care because I just wanted some part of him. I took whatever I could get. I wanted a man who was not only heavily involved with another woman, but one who never respected me, Grace or himself. A couple of days passed before I saw Daniel again and when I did, something fishy was going on.

"She messed your face up. Why do you let her scratch and hit you? You need to have her ass arrested."
"That b*tch is crazy. I just want her out my damn house."
"Daniel if you really wanted her out..."

"She has my damn daughter and threatened to not let me see her." Daniel interrupted me and I heard the pain in his voice.
"That's a chance you need to take."
"I know you cheated, but she has no right to hit and scratch your face like that. You have to work, and people will see you like that. Besides all that, that's just violent and wrong."

I would have loved for Grace to get locked up. That meant I got to spend more time with Daniel. Grace was wrong for the physical violence, and I wanted Daniel to call the police on her. Daniel's skin was literally peeled off his face. The scratch was about two inches long, and I could see his pink flesh. I removed the peroxide from the medicine cabinet and cleaned his wound. Thereafter, I embraced Daniel with a kiss.

"What have you been doing?"
"What do you mean?"
"Your mouth smells like p*ssy."
"I don't know how. I haven't done anything with Grace. Maybe it's because I didn't brush my teeth."
I never asked if you had sex with Grace. I thought.
"Go brush your teeth then. Just gross."
"Shut up man."
Nasty ass bastard, I hope he doesn't think I believe that sh*t. Mouth smells like a nasty ass p*ssy. That's just damn gross. Lying ass. I really need to get rid of him. Just ain't no good. I thought.
Daniel's phone rang.
"Hey Ma, sure I will go. Give me about thirty minutes and I will be there. I'm over Kelley's house. We're not doing much. Okay. I will be there in a minute."
"Kelley I'm going to take Ma to the store. Do you want to go?"
"Sure."
We arrived at Ms. Harris's place and I sat on the couch. For whatever reason, she felt the need to ask if I would drive.
"Do you mind driving Kelley?"
I quickly jumped up from her couch and was ready to give her my keys.

"Slow down. Don't hurt yourself."
"I'll drive."
I didn't want to disappoint Daniel and not be there for his mother. I never forgot his words and how he felt about her. So I was there for her when she was in need. This was the first time I saw Daniel as a Mama's boy. Before we entered Menard's, Ms. Harris stepped out of line and Daniel didn't disagree with her.
"Shh; you're loud."
"I can laugh."
"Just lower your voice."
Daniel agreed with his mother.
"I'm grown and your mother will not tell me how to behave. I'm not her child."
"I know, but you were loud."
"You didn't have a problem with it until she said something."
"Just drop it."
After Ms. Harris finished shopping, I dropped them off and went home. *I don't know who this fat b*tch thinks she is telling me to be quiet. Then his punk ass agreed with her like I was nothing. Mama's boy ass punk.* I thought. I made it home and before I could sit down my phone rang.
"Hello."
"Hi Kelley."
"Who is this?"
"This is Grace."
"How did you get my phone number and why are you calling me?"
"I thought you said you weren't seeing Daniel."
"Don't call my phone with that damn mess. Take that sh*t up with your man."
I hung up and called Daniel.
"Hello."
"Hey Daniel. How did Grace get my phone number? Why is she calling me?"
"I don't know. She might have gone through my phone. Let me call her ass. I will talk to you later."
"Bye."

I decided to go out by myself and was something I did often. I went to the Old 50 Yard Line on seventy-fifth and Michigan. I had too much to drink as I always did. My tolerance for alcohol was very high, and one or two drinks were never enough. I made it home safely after driving drunk. My phone awoke me.
"Hey Daniel."
"Hey baby. After the gym, why don't you come by my house?
"Isn't Grace still there?"
"Nope, I put her out, but she has to come get the rest of her stuff."
"Are you sure that's okay?"
"Yea."

****

"Okay. I will follow you."
"This is a nice house you have."
"Thanks. I packed all her stuff and I'm waiting on her to come get it."
"That's good."
It doesn't look like a home, kind of shabby and not really lived in. She's the woman. What the hell is she doing? This house is nice and it looks like sh*t. I thought.
Night fell and we decided to watch a movie. *The doorbell rang.*
"Stay here."
Daniel looked out the living room window and walked back to the bedroom.
"That's her ass and she can stay out there."
"Maybe I should leave."
"You don't have to leave. She will leave eventually."
Loud, hard bangs came from the kitchen door.
"Damn. She seems mad as hell, banging like that."
"She can bang as long as she wants. She ain't getting in here, f*ck her."
Grace eventually left and I spent a night. The next morning as I was driving home, I saw Grace's car exit the expressway. Moments later I received a phone call.

"Hi Kelley, you thought your p*ssy was better than mine."
"You are one sick ass female."
"I will always f*ck Daniel."
"So will I b*tch, dumb ass."
I hung up the phone and called Daniel.
"Hello Daniel. This female just called me and said, *you thought your p*ssy was better than mine.*"
"Who?"
"Grace."
"Are you serious?"
"Yes, I am. You need to put her in her damn place. I don't want her ass calling me anymore."
"Well cuss her ass out if she calls again."
"Trust me she's going to get an ear full."
"Do what have to because I don't give a sh*t. What the hell is wrong with her? That sh*t was stupid as hell. I will call you back Kelley."
*This b*tch has a lot of nerve calling my damn phone. Stupid ass female.* I thought. Days passed before I saw Daniel again and the next time I visited him, he was packing the rest of Grace's belongings.
"Is this the rest of Grace's stuff?"
"Yea. I'm packing the rest of her sh*t so she can come get it?"
"I can help you."

Daniel had a ranch style home with two bedrooms, a full finished basement, one and a half bathrooms, a back yard, and a large eat-in kitchen. The backyard housed a rosebush that grew into his walkway and stabbed me when I wasn't paying attention. The living room walls were dull white. The carpet was from the early fifties or sixties, shabby and red if I'm not mistaken. Colorful and unattractive wallpaper covered the kitchen wall. Daniel told me he bought the house from an older couple, and based on the looks and decorations, it was clear. I figured after he evicted Grace, we could make his house into a home. I never wanted to move in. I just wanted to help Daniel make his home comfortable. I was foolish to believe I would be comfortable with Daniel, or in his house. He showed me time and time I should have run long before I got started. Daniel's sex, generosity, and abuse addicted me.

"Daniel, are you going to fix your house? You make very good money."
"I am. I just want her out. I don't want her getting too comfortable and enjoying my sh*t. She's has judged me ever since I got that other woman pregnant."
"Let me know if you need some help fixing your place."
"I will."

August 1999
"Hey Anna, this is Daniel. Daniel this is Anna, my friend, we work at the hospital together."
"How are you doing?"
"I'm fine and you?
"I'm good."
"Kelley, you can find a seat. I have to get to the choir."

Greater Mount Hebron was a beautiful, large church. I believe it may have set about two to three hundred people. Pews sat on opposite sides of the aisle, and the floor covered with red carpet gave the church a sense of power. The red carpet led directly to the altar that housed the pulpit. The pulpit was brown and sitting directly behind it were brown pews where the First Lady and deacons sat. To the right and left of the pulpit was the choir section. The sisters sat to the left and the brothers sat to the right. They were all dressed in their black robes with a yellow stole. Pastor Ledbetter was about five feet eleven, medium brown skin with a short Afro. He always dressed nicely in his black or blue suit covered by his black and yellow robe. He was a kind and an awesome pastor who believed in serving God. He performed the eulogy at my father's funeral. Pastor Ledbetter preached his sermon from the pulpit until he decided to join us on the floor section. He was a walking preacher. His presence was so powerful, I wanted him to lay his hands on me. I cried, but these were tears of joy. I stood up, clapped to the music. Daniel sat still in his seat. Before I knew it, an overwhelming feeling took over and the Holy Spirit surfaced. A feeling of joy overwehelmed me. After church we stopped by Nicki's place. I wanted to share my good news with her and Mama. Veto, Nicki's boyfriend was there and Lord knows I couldn't stand the sight of him, and had no reason to speak to him. *I do not like this damn man, raggedy bum ass. I wish Nicki would leave his broke ass.* I thought.

"Girl you look like you high."
"Hey Nicki, I am. I just came from church and finally felt the Holy Spirit. The feeling was like nothing I ever felt."
"I need to go and join somebody's church."
"Yea, you should. Where's Mama?"
"She's upstairs. Okay, I'm going up."
"Hey Mama."
I hugged her as I always did when I visited.
"Hey baby."
"Hey Lionel."
"Hey baby girl."
"Hey Granny and Lionel, how y'all doing?
Daniel hugged Mama and shook Lionel's hand.
"We just came from church and I wanted to see you how you were doing."
"I feel fine. I have a doctor's appointment in the morning. I gotta have a liver biopsy."
"What time is your appointment?"
"At seven in the morning?"
"Okay. I will be here at six fifteen."
"Okay. Thanks baby. How was church?"
"I finally felt the Holy Spirit, and it was a great feeling."
"That's good baby. Don't stop going."
"I'm not. I gotta get going. Daniel and I are going out tonight, but I will be here in the morning."
"Are you sure girl?"
"I will make sure Granny."
"I will be here Mama. I love y'all."

Daniel and I went up North to an alternative club called the Spin on Halsted and Belmont. I shared my interest in women with Daniel and he had no problem introducing me to that lifestyle. We shot pool and had cocktails. Homosexual, lesbian and bisexual people crowded the Spin. I had a good time, and we planned to go back to visit some of the other clubs.
"Let's get out of here."
Daniel was ready to go.
"Okay. That's cool."
"So did you like it?"
"It was cool?"
"So you've never hung out up here."
"Nope, mostly downtown and the city. How do you know about this area?"
"I lived with my stepfather up here for a while when I was younger. There's another area called Boy's Town up here too."
"What is Boy's Town?"
"That's where all the homosexuals hang."
"I'd like to go there one day."
"I will show you. There's another place we're gonna stop at real quick."
"And what is this place?"
"The Pleasure Chest."
"What is the Pleasure Chest?"
"It's a toy shop; adult toy shop. You ain't ever heard of it?"
"Nope."
"Do you have any vibrators?"
"Is that like a dildo?
Laughter from Daniel
"Something like that, but women use them to masturbate. They use it on their clitoris."
"Nope, I don't have one and ain't ever used one. I used a dildo once or twice in my shows when I was a dancer."
"This is the Pleasure Chest."
Daniel pulled up and parked.
"I've been to this adult shop on seventy-six and Cicero, but I can't remember the name. They sold more adult movies than anything."

We walked into the Pleasure Chest and I was outdone by all the sex toys I saw.
"These are vibrators Kelley. Get one."
"Alright I have one."
"Okay, let me pay for it and we can go."

Daniel purchased my first vibrator and wanted me to use it in the car and I did. I would have probably done anything he asked me to do. He was so nice and generous and I didn't want to lose him. I was willing to lose myself to keep him. This was the beginning of my life as a bisexual woman. We rarely partied at any clubs on the South side of Chicago. Practically every Wednesday or weekend, we were on the North side hanging out and meeting women. We were regulars at the Spin, the Closet and many other gay bars. I lusted for women and it got to a point where I went to the North side by myself and Daniel had no idea. It didn't stop at the clubs. Daniel introduced me to the chat line where we could talk to and, meet women. I had no idea what I was getting myself into.
"Now go ahead and try it."
"What do I do?"
"Just put it on your clitoris and tell me how it feels."
I did what Daniel said, but I was really embarrassed so I stopped.
"How did it feel?"
"It felt okay."
"Now you know what a vibrator is."
We made it to my place, and as I exited the car, Daniel didn't.
"Are you coming in?"
"Naw, I gotta get home."
"Okay, see you later."

I was still mentally unstable and lacked self-love. I knew Daniel was still seeing Grace and I accepted it. I was accustomed to this type of betrayal, and really didn't give two nickels about Grace. I felt like if Daniel wanted to see me, then I was going to see him. Who cares if she got hurt? He always told me she cheated on him anyway. He also said he didn't want her anymore and she was no good. So I felt like she got what she deserved.

"Hello."

"Hey Daniel, are you busy?"

"Hey Kelley, naw I'm not."

Daniel sounded sad.

"Is it okay if I stop by?"

"Yea, I'm here."

The front door was open when I arrived, and Daniel was cleaning his house.

"Kelley I can't see you anymore."

"Why not?"

"I need to get some things straight with Grace and make sure that door is closed before I start something with you."

"No, No, No."

I dropped to the floor and laid on the red, shabby carpet in the hallway that led to the kitchen.

"Get off the floor Kelley."

"Why do we have to stop seeing each other?"

"Because this is too much drama. I need to clear my head and figure some things out. Grace is trying to keep my daughter away from me."

"Okay."

I cried and Daniel told me he would be in touch. I left, went home and continued on with my day. I didn't understand why Daniel wanted to break up with me. We had only dated for about three months. Whenever I called Daniel, he rarely answered the phone and I assumed it was because he was with Grace. Although Daniel told me we couldn't see each other anymore, he didn't keep his word. After a couple of weeks passed, Daniel called and we continued to see each other. He told me things weren't going to work out with Grace so he stopped seeing her. I actually believed him.

September 1999

"Hello."

"Hey Kelley, are you ready?"

"Yep."

"I'm on my way."
Daniel and I went to the gym as we always did. Our workouts were very intense and fulfilling. He taught me a lot about weight training and defining my muscles.
"That was a good workout. Are you coming by my place now?"
I wanted Daniel to come home with me. I always wanted him.
"Yea sure."
"So who was the light-skinned guy?"
"That was my boy Nate. We work together."
"He's a good-looking guy."
"Would you do him?"
"Not by myself. If we had a threesome."
"Hmmph. So you would sleep with my boy?"
"If we were together."
"So what you want to f*ck him?"
"Don't switch sh*t up. I said the only way is if we had a threesome."
"Why would I want to f*ck you with my boy? Ain't none of you b*tches sh*t. All you mother*ckers are wh*res!"
"What the f*ck is wrong with you? You asked and I answered."
"F*ck that sh*t bi*ch. Wh*re. Motherf*cker!"
"You must think you're talking to Grace because I haven't done sh*t to you. What the f*ck? Don't call me out of my name again."
"F*ck you b*tch."
"You're a stupid bastard. Trifling, disrespectful ass motherf*cker."
"Take me the f*ck home and shut the f*ck up talking to me!"
"B*tch I'm not taking you nowhere. I'm going the f*ck home."
"You're going to take me home b*tch."
"Wait and see."
This nigga took that conversation way to the left and showed me a side of him that I never seen. I really don't understand his anger toward me. I only answered his question truthfully, and this is what I get. I thought. I knew his anger wasn't directed at me. I could understand why he got upset, but that was a bit much. Daniel was angry about what he and Grace were going through and all I did was add fuel to the fire. Nevertheless, I did not deserve that mess.

"B*tch take me home!"
I ignored Daniel. *He got to get the hell out my car. I don't understand what I did to deserve this type of treatment. If that b*tch is making him so miserable, why the f*ck is he still involved. Only four months passed and everything seemed very well. He ain't ever talked to me like this.* I thought. I pulled up to my place in Calumet Park, parked my car, got out and walked toward my building.
"B*tch, you need to take me home!"
"F*ck you. What the f*ck are you doing? Leave my car alone."
"Now b*tch. Since you won't take me home, let see if you drive anywhere else."
"What the f*ck did you do to my car?"
"Take me the f*ck home now!"
"I'm not taking your ignorant ass anywhere. I will call the police."
"Nine one one where's your emergency?"
"Can you send a police officer to 12732 S. Aberdeen? My boyfriend just went under the hood of my car and disconnected something and now it won't start."
"Where is he now?"
"He just ran through the parking lot."
"What does he look like? I'm dispatching the officers now."
"He's about six feet tall, medium complexion, light brown eyes, medium athletic build, and he's wearing some blue uniform pants and a burgundy, hooded sweatshirt."
"Okay the officers are on their way now."
"Thank you."
I stood outside for about five minutes and the two officers walked up.
"Did you call the police?"
"Yes, I did."
"What's your name?"
"Kelley Porter."
"Do you have some I.D?"
"Yes."
"What happened?"

"Me and my boyfriend got into an argument and he called me all kinds of names so I refused to take him home. Then he disconnected something on my car because it won't start."
"Where does he live?"
"On one hundred twenty-sixth and Damen"
"That's down the street. He can just walk."
"That's what I told him."
"You can sign this report and if he comes back, call us."
"Thank you."
Before I could get to the second floor, my phone rang.
"Hello."
"Why did you call the police on me?"
"What did you do to my car? What did you do? You had no right to treat me like you did. I didn't do anything to you and I didn't deserve that."
"Come downstairs."
"Downstairs. Are you outside?"
"Yea, I took the Distributor Cap off."
"Well put it back."
"Pop the hood. You can start it."
F*cking asshole. I thought. Daniel got in the car, and I really didn't have much to say to him. I dropped him off and pulled off. I didn't understand why he would treat me the way he did. We partied a lot together and never had any arguments. The most he did was stress about his relationship with Grace and how he impregnated another woman. He didn't speak much of this woman, and later I learned why. The next day Daniel called to apologize.
"Hello."
"Hey Kelley, I wanted to apologize to you. I was wrong and I'm just sick of Grace's ass. I wish she would just leave me the f*ck alone."
"Stop sleeping with her Daniel."
"I haven't slept with her ass in a while."
"I don't know what to tell you, but thanks for apologizing."
"What are you doing later?"
"Nothing."
"Let's go up north."
"That's cool."

Daniel lied all the time about not sleeping with Grace. I knew he was. Maybe he did stop from time to time, but he never cut Grace off completely until years later. Daniel failed to realize as long as they slept together, the emotional attachment would always be there. Nevertheless, their relationship never stopped me from dating Daniel. I learned later there was only one thing that would bring our relationship to a complete halt.

Cheating Bisexual – 2

December 1999
"What about her over there Daniel?" I think she's interested. She keeps staring at me."
"Which one?"
"The white girl with the short haircut; she's wearing the blue overall. She's on the other side of the pool table."
"I see her. She's cute. Go say something to her."
"Okay."

The Spin was an alternative club that catered to lesbians, bisexual, homosexuals and transgender people. Not to say heterosexual people didn't frequent the place, but when they did, I always questioned their motives. Although Daniel said he lived up north with his step-father for a while, I also questioned him. Upon entering the Spin, it housed a bar to the right of the entrance door. The bar circled the Spin from one side to the other. Towards the back were two pool tables and if you turn right, there was a DJ booth along with a big screen TV that displayed the videos with the matching music. Directly to the left of the TV was an entrance to another section where people danced and made out or entertainment took the stage. But that's not where my sexual encounters took place. My encounters at the Spin were always in the bathroom not far from the bar, but on the opposite side of the entrance. I lusted for women, but not all women. I preferred women who didn't look like me. I wanted the total opposite of me. Women who were White, Asian or Hispanic, and throughout the course of this confusing time for me, I had sex with all. It really didn't matter where. I had to fill that deep, dark, lustful sin that lived beneath my skin. I wasn't happy with me, hated me and very confused about my identity. I looked good on the outside and appeared highly confident and secure.

Underneath all that glamour, jewelry, make-up, nice clothing, and a chiseled body, I was a twenty-nine year old female still mentally lost, confused, lacked self-love and was good at self-betrayal. The abuse, although forgiven; left me in total crisis of who I was, and to become. All I knew at that time was I was in love with Daniel and overpowered by the lust I had for women. This particular night when I embarked upon a desire in my body that felt like a caged animal. Thereafter, the "Seed of Betrayal" developed into a tree, and I spiraled out of control.

"Hi. I'm Kelley."
I smiled as I looked her up and down.
She was about five feet two inches, Hispanic, short haircut, brown eyes, nice perky breasts, and a medium build. I looked at her with lust and imagined the things I would do to her.
"Hello. I'm Cassandra. How are you?"
"I'm fine. Are you here with someone?"
"A few friends, they went to get drinks?"
"Do you all want to play me and my friend in a game of pool?"
"Sure. That would be fun."
"Daniel this is Cassandra."
"Hey. How are you?"
"Cassandra this is my friend Daniel."
"It's nice to meet you Daniel?
I referred to Daniel as my friend since we knew some women would be less likely to engage with us if they knew he was my man. Cassandra's friends made it back and she introduced us to them. We all made small talk, but I focused on Cassandra.
"Where are you from?"
Cassandra moved a little closer to me.
"I'm from Chicago, but I live in the Suburbs."
"What about you?"
"I'm from Chicago, but I live on the North side."
"What are you doing after you leave from here?"
"I'm going home."
"How about you come home with us?"
"I would like that, but is Daniel coming? I'm not interested in him."
"Are you interested in me?"
"Yes, I am."
"He can just watch, or join in if you change your mind?"
"I've been with men before, but I prefer women today."

"I understand. But since he and I date from time to time and I came with him, he has to at least be in the room or he's not going to let you come with us."
"Okay. That's fine. Let me tell my friends I'm going with you and then we can leave."
I watched her as she walked away and really could not wait to get her home with me. I knew Daniel would be involved, but I really didn't want him there.
"What did she say Kelley?"
"I got her. She's going to tell her friends that she's leaving with us."
"Cool."
Intoxicated, reckless, and driving about seventy miles per hour on Lake Shore, all I could think about was indulging in this woman completely. The first time was for about five minutes and really an experiment. This was what my body craved for over fifteen years. My body never forgot the pleasure of kissing and grinding girls and this night would be the beginning of something I couldn't imagine.
"Stop driving so fast."
Cassandra looked at me in the rear-view mirror.
"You are reckless."
Daniel agreed.
I looked in my rear view mirror and smiled at Cassandra. I slowed down and blasted the music. We finally made it home.
"Daniel, we're going to take a shower."
"Okay, I will be right here waiting. I need some popcorn."
Cassandra and I laughed. She followed me into the bathroom, undressed and stepped into the shower. We began to kiss and touch each other. *This is exactly what I wanted. She has nice lips and titties.* I thought. Cassandra followed me to my bedroom. Daniel sat in my wicker chair next to my black lacquer dresser with plenty of perfume on it. Cassandra joined me on my full size bed covered with a black and gray blanket. My first real experience began with a woman. I had been with two men before, but not a man and woman. Daniel watched for a while.
"I wanna join. Shit. Y'all look good as hell."
Cassandra and I looked at each other.

"Is it okay Cassandra?"
"Yeah, it's fine."
Daniel got into bed with us and he was so excited he couldn't maintain his erection. I assumed he was upset that I was more involved with Cassandra than I was with him. His face frowned and eventually he stuck his d*ck in Cassandra and his frown disappeared. Daniel's actions while inside of Cassandra were very malicious as if he was trying to make me jealous, and he did. I told him to come out of her. He stuck his d*ck in me and I didn't want him. I only wanted Cassandra. Daniel became upset again after noticing I wasn't interested in him. He left and went home. Cassandra and I continued on until the wee hours of the morning, we drove to Daniel's house. *The doorbell rang.*

"Why did you leave?"
"I wasn't getting anything out of it."
"Come back to the house with us."
"Naw, I'm good."
"You have a nice house Daniel."
"Thanks."

"Okay, see you later."
Cassandra and I laughed as we walked toward the door. We went back to my place and that "Seed of Betrayal" took over again. The rest of the night was moaning and me powerless to the lust. The worst part was, the entire act was without the use of any protection. The next morning I was so ready for Cassandra to leave my house. I knew I wasn't a lesbian or bisexual. I was powerless and confused. *Why is she taking so damn long to get dressed? I wish she would hurry the hell up so I can drop her off.* I thought.
"Where do I need to drop you off?"
"Downtown, I'm going straight to work."
"Okay. I'm going to start the car up, and I will be right back."
It was about thirty degrees outside, but the sun was shining. I started the car and went back upstairs. Cassandra was finally ready.

"You were good."
Cassandra placed her hands between my legs.
"Girl you're gonna make me crash."
"Will I see you again?"
"Yea, that's fine Cassandra. You were good too."
"Here is my phone number. Make sure you call me."
"Okay, I will."

Cassandra exited my car and I pulled off. I drove to Daniel's house and he wasn't home. I called his phone and no answer. I went home, took a shower and thought about the entire night. I laughed out loud since Daniel wasn't able to keep his erection. *That felt good and I can't wait to do it again. She knew exactly what she was doing. Too bad Daniel couldn't stay up. Oh well. I enjoyed myself.* I thought. I enjoyed that experience beyond my understanding. What was to come afterwards was complete and utter disrespect, whorish, dangerous, and confusion at its worst.

A few days later, Cassandra invited me to a house party. I dressed in my green suede pants and vest with my green cowboy boots. When I entered the apartment, there was one man and plenty of women. The apartment was small and filled with bisexual, lesbians, marijuana, cigarette smoke and alcohol. The living room housed a dark brown two piece living room set; a love seat and sofa. There was a brown cocktail table sitting in front of the sofa with a fish bowl on it and no fish.
"Hi Kelley."
"Hi Cassandra."
"Everybody this is Kelley."
"Hello."
I was somewhat uncomfortable.
"I will be right back."
Cassandra walked in the kitchen.
"Okay."
I had never been to an intimate party as this one. I really didn't know how to behave so I stood off to the side by myself.

"What's up girl? I see you came out tonight. I didn't think you were going to make it."
"Hey Charles, it's good to see you again."
"You too."
Charles was Cassandra's friend. I wasn't certain if he was gay or straight. He was black, about five feet five with a round, plump frame, and wore a short Afro. I never connected why he hung out with so many lesbians and bisexual women. I wasn't really familiar with anyone but Cassandra and Charles so after a while, I decided to get a drink. I figured I would relax a bit. Several women stood in the door opening that lead to the kitchen. I wasn't attracted to black women, and I didn't understand why Cassandra was the only Hispanic woman there. I wondered who she knew besides Charles.
"Excuse me."
The women stepped to the side and as I entered the kitchen, I saw Cassandra cornered with another woman. I looked at her and proceeded to get my drink.
"Kelley, this is my friend Stacy."
"Hi Stacy."
"Hi."
Stacy looked me up and down with a frown on her face. As Cassandra walked toward my way, Stacy rubbed her ass. I wasn't upset at all. I was more bored and irritated. I went to the bathroom to get away from them. I felt really uncomfortable and confused about why I was there.
"Who is it?"
"It's Cassandra."
I opened the bathroom door and let her in. She immediately started kissing me and I pulled away from her.
"What are you doing? I don't need any problems. Isn't that your girlfriend?"
"No. She was my girlfriend and she wants to get back with me."
"Oh. Okay."
"So can I come to your place tonight?"
"I don't think that would be a good idea."

I grabbed the door knob, but before I could exit, Cassandra kissed me again and I wanted her. But, I was so uncomfortable in this place, I left.
"I will talk to you later."
"Okay."

I don't know why I came to this party. All those black women. I'm not even attracted to black women. I wonder what Daniel is doing. Maybe I will give him a call. I will not go to another house party she invites me too. I thought. I called Daniel and he blew me off several times. I didn't understand what he was mad at. I stopped calling him, went home and went to sleep. My phone rang early in the morning.
"Hello."
"Hey Kelley."
"Grace what do you want?"
"Stop calling my man."
"Tell your man to stop calling me."
"Dyke ass b*tch!"
I hung the phone up and was in complete disbelief. *Why would he tell her? I can't believe he told her.* I thought. I was very hurt by that and wanted to retaliate so I did. One of Daniel's brothers was Kevin. He and I talked a lot about his problems as well as Grace and Daniel. Kevin was about five feet six, brown skin, wore glasses, overweight and had a nice personality.
The phone rang.

"Hello."
"Hey Kevin."
"Hey."
"Why is your brother telling people I'm a lesbian?"
"He told me a few things about what y'all did."
"Really, Grace just called talking sh*t and called me a dyke. I know his black ass told her. Let me tell you what really happened. He i mad because he had two naked women in bed and his d*ck wouldn't stay up so he ran out mad."
"He told me some things, but it wasn't like that."
Kevin laughed.

"I'm sure it wasn't. He's never going to tell the truth. Damn liar. That's all I wanted so I will talk to you later."
"Alright."
*His ass is just mad and jealous because he knows I enjoyed her more than I enjoyed him. I'm sure Grace and Kevin were not the only people he told. B*tch. That will never happen again. Ungrateful bastard.* I thought.
Almost a week passed since I talked to or saw Daniel after our threesome.
"Hello."
"Hey Kelley."
"Hey Daniel."
"What's wrong with you?"
"Why did you tell Grace about what we did?"
"I didn't tell her sh*t."
"How did she know?"
"Sh*t, I don't know. She's just trying to pick you and find out if we've been together. Maybe she's just trying to hurt your feelings."
"Whatever Daniel, I know your ass told her; lying bastard."
I hung the phone up.
"What?!"
"Why did you hang up?"
"Because I know your ass is lying."
"Kelley I didn't tell her anything. Maybe she said it because she wants to sleep with you. Sh*t, she's been there."
"Whatever."
"I'm on my way over there."
"Bye."
I looked off the balcony and rolled my eyes at Daniel. *I really don't even know why he brought his black ass over here. Lying dog.* I thought.
"Hey."
"Girl let it go. I told you I didn't tell her nothing."
"I know you did, but it doesn't matter. F*ck her. If she calls my phone one more time I'm going to hurt her damn feelings."
"Do it then. F*ck her. Now give me some."

Daniel and I went in my bedroom and he did what he usually did; please my body in ways I never felt. I believe I was in love with his sex. How could I love someone who treated me like garbage? I definitely didn't love myself. I was really lost. To date a man with a woman was one thing, but to date a man who was willing to sleep with another woman in my presence didn't say much about me. But Daniel asked for it and I would have given him just about anything in return for his love. He was a lying, cheating, disrespectful womanizer who didn't care about any woman, but his mother.
"Kelley, do you want to go get something to eat?"
"Sure."
Daniel and I went to the Egg Shack to have breakfast. Egg Shack was a small restaurant in Calumet Park. The food was always great and the people were very nice. Thereafter, we went back home, had sex again and watched TV.

Daniel's phone rang.
"Hey Ma, I'm with Kelley. Okay. I will be there in a few minutes."
"Are you leaving?"
"Yea, my mother needs me to run her somewhere."
"Where is Steven?"
"He's there, but he doesn't do sh*t."
"Oh. Are you coming back?"
"I will call you and we can go out later."
Why is she even with that nigga if he can't do anything for her? Why does she always call Daniel and what does she think we're doing early in the morning. I thought. I really had no idea how close Daniel and his mother were. I knew from hearsay he was her favorite son and would do anything for her.

Blocked incoming call
"Hello."
"Hi Kelley."
"What the f*ck do you want?"
"Daniel told me you lost your job."
"So what and why the f*ck are you calling me?"

"That's what you get b*tch?"
"F*ck you, you gray teeth b*tch."
I hung the phone up and called Daniel.
"Hello."
"Hey Daniel, did you tell Grace I got laid off?"
"Hell naw."
"How did she know? You are the only person who knew."
I didn't tell her sh*t and I don't know how she found out."
"Why did she call my phone telling me you told her?"
"Kelley I didn't tell her sh*t. Why the f*ck would I tell her that?"
"I really don't know, but I'm tired of her ass calling me. Silly ass female."
"Kelley I promise I didn't tell her. You didn't like the job anyway, right? So don't worry about that sh*t. I will find out how she knew. Let me call you back."
*This bi*ch is sick out of her mind calling and stalking me. I never understood a woman who approached another female about a man, especially if she wasn't married. That is the dumbest sh*t ever. I thought.*

The phone rang.
"Hey Daniel."
"Hey Kelley, I know how she found out about you being laid off."
"How?"
"Somehow her stupid ass got the password to my phone and checked my messages. When I asked her, she told me she knew people who you knew."
"I know that's a lie because first of all, she doesn't know anyone I know and I haven't told anyone but you."
"I know. Do me a favor."
"Call my phone and say you got a call back from another job and the starting pay is seventeen dollars an hour. I bet she won't call you telling you that sh*t. She broke as hell and been doing hair all her life and ain't got sh*t. She only works three days a week, but her ass is always at the gym. She thought I was going to marry her ass. She had the nerve to go buy a wedding dress and try it on."

"For real."

"Hell yeah."

"I ain't marrying her ass. I don't even trust her ass. I believe she was f*cking one of the workers at CTA. I caught her in the pool with some dude at the gym. She was in his arms and when I asked her about it, she told me he was teaching her how to swim. I don't trust that b*tch."

"That's messed up. I don't know many women who would allow a man so close unless she's interested."

"That's what I said. I'm on my over there to get you so we can go to the North side."

"Okay."

I was happy he dogged Grace out and didn't trust her. I figured if he didn't want to marry her, maybe he wanted to marry me. It made me feel good when he criticized and belittled her. Somehow I believed he no longer wanted Grace.

At the Spin, we met a young woman who was more than willing to have sex with both of us. She was black and I wasn't turned on by black women. But we went into the bathroom and Daniel and I both doused her body with our tongues. She wanted to go home with us, but we refused. On many occasions, I went up north by myself seeking women. If I wasn't up north, I called the chat line. I slept with some of the women I met and some I didn't. I was completely powerless, and every time I indulged in a woman's body, I wanted more. The experience I received was not enough and I never stopped seeking or lusting until I got exactly what I desired. Daniel and I made it home at around three o'clock in the morning. We were both too drunk to stand up straight.

I thought I hit the jackpot with Daniel and was completely wrong. Daniel was a comedian at heart who kept me laughing. He trusted and was very proud of me. He also told me many times that he would marry me if he didn't have so much baggage. I only saw the good in Daniel. I ignored his cheating behaviors, his careless sexual appetite, his verbally abusive mouth and his Mama's boy mentality. I actually thought he was a good man. He was about as good as I was. We were two broken, and dysfunctional abused souls who wreaked havoc on each other. Daniel was incapable of fully committing to one woman. I along with Grace was heartbroken. Based on Daniel's behavior and his relationship with his mother, I am certain he experienced some form of childhood abuse.

I really didn't care about Grace and had no remorse for causing her pain. I figured when Daniel got that other woman pregnant, she should have left him, but she stayed knowing he cheated on her. So why would I care about her feelings? Not to mention, I was unhappy so causing someone else pain was nothing to me. I was still confused about my sexuality, my self-esteem was low, and I had no respect for Daniel or Grace. The entire relationship was extremely toxic, sexual and dysfunctional. For whatever reason, Daniel never told his mother *no* when she needed him.

"Hi Ms. Harris."
"Hi Kelley, how are you?"
"I'm fine."
"Let me use the bathroom Ma."
Ms. Harris and I waited on the front porch, and talked about the argument Daniel and I had.
"He called me every name in the book. He called me a b*tch, wh*re, slut, motherf*cker and."
"My son said all that to you? He wasn't talking to you. He was talking to her." Ms. Harris politely interrupted me.

I sat and listened to her advice and at the end of the conversation her exact words were, *everything will work out the way it should. He should not have started something with you until he closed the door on her.*

After we left Ms. Harris's house, Daniel and I went out later that night seeking women. We went to the Berlin night club which was down the street from the Spin. As we approached Berlin, there was plenty of pop, heavy metal and techno music echoing from the club walls to the streets. We walked in and the disco lights shined on the men who gyrated their pelvic areas in front of those who watched. It was kind of strange to not see any women watching. Plenty of black and white shirtless men danced closely upon each other, women kissing, and others jumping around to the beat of the music. Daniel and I walked to the bar and ordered a drink. We watched for a moment, and then our night began. I felt comfortable in this surrounding. I was comfortable lusting over women, kissing them, rubbing their breast and grinding their bodies on the dance floor. I was also very much attracted to Daniel, but around a White, Hispanic or Asian woman, Daniel meant nothing. We danced and rolled our bodies into each other and I noticed a woman staring at me.

"Check her out Daniel."
"Who?"
"The white blonde over your shoulder. She is staring pretty hard. I can't tell if she wants me or you."
"Go find out."
I danced my way over to her.
"Hi. Are you having fun?
"Hi. I will be if you dance with me."
I looked over at Daniel to make sure it was okay and he nodded his head. Daniel had no idea how much I wanted women and if he knew better, he would have never introduced me to the North side or the chat line.
"What's your name?!"
"Beth!"
"My name is Kelley!"
"I've always wanted a beautiful black woman. You look like a model."
"Thank you Beth. You're very pretty."
"Kelley I have to go to the bathroom. Do you want to come with me?"
"Sure. Daniel I'm going to the bathroom, I will be right back."
"Okay."

Beth and I approached the bathroom and there was a tall white guy standing at the door. I wondered why they needed security to guard the bathroom.
"One at a time!"
The security guard yelled at two men trying to go in the bathroom together so Beth and I snuck into the ladies bathroom. We immediately began kissing and I lifted her shirt and kissed her breast. We were very into each other. She rubbed between my thighs and pulled my pants down. She dropped to her knees and licked my p*ussy as I stood there with my pants on the floor. The door opened, I looked up and smiled.
"Come on. Pull your clothes up and let's go."
"Okay."
He shut the door behind him and we kissed again.
"We're coming out now."
The security guard banged on the bathroom door. We exited the bathroom smiling, and as we walked toward Daniel, I noticed how he observed our locked hands.
"Where were y'all at?"
"Waiting to use the bathroom, there was a line."
From Daniel's position he was unable to gain a visual of the bathroom. There was a wall that separated the club and the bathroom, and he was standing directly behind it from afar.

"Let's get another drink. So what's up with her?"
"Her name is Beth and nothing now. I haven't had a chance to really talk to her."
"Oh. Okay."
"I will introduce you to her."
"Cool."
"Can I have two Long Island Iced Teas?"

That was Daniel's first Long Island. He didn't drink as much as I did and it was funny to see his face after his first sip. I assumed men knew how to drink or they knew about a Long Island. Daniel somehow didn't. I was feeling pretty good. Daniel and I danced until we were sweating as if we had just left the gym. He wasn't a good dancer, but he blended in very well. The most he did was move his feet from the front to back and gyrate his penis area. On the other hand, I was certainly a dancer. My favorite dance move blended in well. I threw my leg up in the air and once it landed back on the ground, I did a one-eighty spin with my arms out to the side. That was one of those house moves and all these men were very familiar with that move. It almost appeared as a gay man's dance move. I really enjoyed dancing on the north side because it was pure freedom for me.

"Beth, this is Daniel."
"How are you?"
"I'm good."
"So who are you here with?"
"My roommate."
"That's cool."
"Y'all wanna dance."

Daniel smiled at me and walked towards the dance floor. Beth looked at me for approval as we walked toward the dance floor. We sandwiched her, but she and I couldn't keep our hands to ourselves. We kissed and rubbed on each other. We weren't the only ones freak dancing on the floor. There were plenty of men kissing and bending each other over as well as women dancing and kissing. Beth, Daniel and I danced to at least two more songs, and I could tell she wasn't interested in him. I really didn't care because at that point, I wasn't interested in him either. Beth was white, about five feet four inches with a very nice body. She had long brown hair and was wearing blue jeans with a fitted white shirt. She was hot and I was anxious to sleep with her.

"Can I come home with you?"
"Yes, but what are we going to do with your friend? My roommate is a guy and he's gay. I don't know if your friend wants to hang with him, but I want you."
"I will ask him."

There ain't no damn way Daniel is even interested in being with a man, but maybe he can pretend so that I can go home with her. I wonder if he will agree. I thought.

"Beth wants us to come home with her and she said her roommate is gay and I know that's not you so what do you want to do?"
"Is she interested in giving me some?"
"I didn't ask her, but I will."
"Yea, go ask her and let's take it from there."
I eased my way through the crowded dance floor and back to Beth. I noticed so many sexy women and rubbed on a few of their asses.
"So what did he say?"
"He wants to know if you're interested in a threesome."
"Not really, but maybe."

I was in pure lust of Beth as I looked at her. We began to kiss again and worked our way through the crowd, and back to the bathroom. At this time Daniel was busy dancing or at least I thought he was. The night was coming to an end, and Beth and I were going home together.

"Kelley I'm going to find my roommate so I will meet you at the front door."
"Okay."
Berlin was crowded and it was difficult to walk through. Every step I took was elbow to elbow.
"Where were you at?"
"Looking for you."
"Yea right, I saw you walk off with that b*tch."
"You wanted to know if she would sleep with both of us so I asked her."
"What did she say?"
"She said she didn't mind."
"Yea, okay."
"She asked me to meet her at the front door."
"Okay. We're leaving."

Daniel pulled me through the crowd and I felt the anger in his hand.
"There she is."
I waved my hand at Beth.
"F*ck this sh*t. Let's go."
"What's wrong?"
"Nothing. Let's just go. Ain't nobody gonna be waiting on her ass. If she wanted to go, she'd be right here."
"She's right there, coming through the crowd."
"Whatever. Let's go."
Daniel and I left and he was pissed. *Jealous bastard. I wanted her and his black ass is cock-blocking. That's okay. The next time I come up here it will be without him.* I thought.

As we walked East on Halsted towards our car, we passed so many fine women and I flirted with one of them. I rubbed another woman's ass and smiled afterward. I was very aggressive and wanted what I wanted, and didn't give two cents about Daniel's feelings. The "Seed of Betrayal" had finally taken over and every day I wanted to come up North and find women to have sex with. I took pleasure in pleasing women sexually. I enjoyed kissing them and their bodies. I was out of control. Cheating on Daniel with another woman was nothing to me. I never cheated with a man, but I definitely had a few women behind his back. I wanted to live a bisexual life and for the first time, I felt no shame about wanting to, or sleeping with women. Of course I didn't walk around announcing my sexual preference, but it became increasingly known to others.

"Ouch. That sh*t hurts. What the hell is wrong with you?"
I snatched my hand away from Daniel's.
"You ain't gon' disrespect me?"
"This is what your ass wanted so now you're mad."
"This is what we wanted, but you will not disrespect me."
"I'm sorry."
"It's cool. Let's just go home."
"What are we doing for the New Year?"
"I don't have any plans?"

"Do you want to go to a party?"
"I don't do those hotel parties. It's too overrated and too many people."
"What do you usually do on New Year's?"
"My momma usually has a party at her house, but I'm not sure if she will this year."
*Whatever, your ass going is to Grace, and that's fine. I will go hang out with Cassandra. F*ck it. Sorry ass men. Ain't none of them sh*t. I guess he'd rather bring the New Year in with her than me. Oh well.* I thought. We made it home and went to sleep. The next morning Daniel went home and I planned on calling the chat line.

My phone rang.
"Hello."
"Hey Kelley, how are you doing girl?"
"Hi Cassandra, I'm fine and you."
"I'm wonderful."
"What's up?"
"I called to invite you to a New Year's party as my date."
"Really?"
"Yes."
"Where is it?"
"It's downtown."
"I will go."
"How is Daniel?"
"He's okay."
"Girl that night was funny and he was really upset."
"Tell me about it."
"Girl you are good. You made me feel so good. I want some more of you."
"That's good to hear."
"Call me later and I will give you all the details for the party."
"Alright cool."

I really wasn't interested in going to any party with Cassandra, and definitely not as her date. I wanted Daniel, but he always wanted his mama. I called his phone a few times and he never answered so I decided to call the chat line and meet some women.

"Hi Sue. Where do you want to meet?"
"We can meet by the McDonald's on one hundred nineteenth and Western."
"Okay. I will be there in fifteen minutes."

It always amazed me when a woman described herself on the phone as some hot chick, but when I saw her in person; she was the complete opposite of hot. Sue didn't look anything like she described. I told her I would call later, and we would go out. That phone call never happened. I called the chat line again and met another woman.

"Hello."
"Hi Regina, where do you want me to pick you up?"
"I live in the city not far from Hyde Park high school."
"Okay. I'm getting ready now. Give me your address and I'll be on my way. I will call you when I'm outside. What are you wearing so that I will know it's you?"
"I'm wearing a blue jean skirt with a brown fitted top and my hair is long."
"Okay. I'm wearing some blue jeans and a pink top. I'm driving a burgundy Oldsmobile Achieva with dark tinted windows. So I will see you in a minute."

The phone rang.
"Hi, may I speak to Regina?"
"This is she."
"This is Kelley. I'm outside."
"Okay. I'm coming out."

Regina came outside and wasn't as pretty as she claimed on the chat line. She was also a black woman. I knew that when I chatted with her, but my body desired the touch of a woman. We made it home and she immediately began kissing and undressing me. She said she was a giver and not a receiver and I was happy about that. She began to lick my p*ssy and I really enjoyed her tongue. I didn't want her to stop. I told her to keep going and she did. My phone rang and I ignored it. Daniel called and I wasn't interested in talking. Regina continued to make me feel good, and I kissed her breast. I wasn't interested in kissing her on the mouth.

My phone rang again.
"Shh, be quiet for a minute Regina. Hey Daniel."
"Why aren't you answering your phone?"
"I was in the tub."
"Yea right, you better not be playing with women."
"Boy please."
"Call me when you get out of the tub."
"Okay."
Regina's head was right back between my thighs and I wanted more and more. I was so overwhelmed by the touch of a woman and being with a woman, I completely lost control. I lusted for women and gave in to the power of the "Seed of Betrayal." I took a shower and dropped Regina off. She wanted to see me again, but I wasn't interested. In my mind it was on to the next woman.

New Year's Eve 1999
The New Year arrived, but Daniel and I didn't have plans to go out. I planned on attending Cassandra's party and by seven pm that I was ready. I cut my hair low weeks before, and colored it blonde. I dressed in my black, fitted, sleeveless dress with a slit on the side. Silver sequence outlined my dress and I wore matching silver jewelry with silver stilettos. There was no snow and it was about thirty degrees outside.
"Hello."
"Hi Cassandra."
"Hey Kelley."
"What's the address of the party?"
"It's a company New Year's party and it's located in my office building."
"What time are you going?"
"I'm on my way there."

"Okay. I will leave out in thirty minutes and meet you there."
"Okay. See you soon."
"Yep, bye."

I really didn't want to go to her party. I wanted Daniel and all I could think about was him being with Grace and how badly I felt. He hadn't called all day and never answered any of my phone calls.

I made it to Cassandra's party and there were plenty of Whites and Hispanics. I was probably one of six black people. I tried to enjoy myself, but all I could do was to check my cell phone to see if Daniel called. The glass chandeliers caught my eyes along with the tables dressed in beautiful sheer, red and white cloth. The white, sheer curtains exposed the skyline of Chicago. The furniture was beautiful. There was plenty of food spread across the eight foot tables and plenty of women and men standing around laughing and talking in their evening gowns and suits.

"Hey girl, you look beautiful."
Cassandra opened her arms to hug me. We were face to face and she tried to kiss me, and I turned my face to the right. I assumed everyone knew she was a lesbian, but I wasn't prepared to show public display of affection to a woman.
"What's wrong?"
"Nothing, I don't believe in public display of affection. Come to the bathroom with me."
We locked our lips and began fondling each other in the stall. I was ready to take her home with me, but I couldn't get Daniel out of my mind.
"Cassandra what are you doing when the party is over?"
"I hope I'm coming home with you."
The phone rang before I could respond.
"Hello."
"Hey Kelley."
"Hey Daniel."
"What are you doing?"
"I'm at a party with some friend's downtown."

"Okay. Why don't you stop by Mama's when you're done? She's having a party?"
"Why don't you put some clothes on and come down here?"
"Naw, I don't do parties like that."
"Parties like what?"
"Like the hotel parties."
"This isn't a hotel party."
"If you wanna stop by, just come when you're done."
"Okay. That's cool. Bye."

I really didn't want to go to his mother's house party. I wanted to enjoy Daniel alone on New Year's Eve. I had mixed emotions and wanted to run the hell out of that party and go be with Daniel, but I wanted Cassandra. We locked lips again and Cassandra kissed on my neck and breast as she pulled my dress down. I wanted her, but I stopped her before she reached my navel.

"Girl let's go back out and have a cocktail."
"Okay."
We drank and danced. I began to lust after some of the other women who were present. I was totally confused. The men were just as fine and sexy, but I was only interested in the women.
"Hey Cassandra."
"Hey Tasha, Tasha this is my friend Kelley."
"How are you? I love your hair."
"Thank you."
"Kelley, I will be right back."
Cassandra went to talk to some other friends.
"Kelley, I'm going to the bar do you want something to drink?"
"Sure. I'll walk with you."
I was already tipsy from the three shots I had with Cassandra.
"Here is your shot."
"Thank you. I have to go to the bathroom."
"I will walk with you."

Tasha followed behind me. I re-did my make-up and Tasha kissed on my neck. I turned around and kissed her. Cassandra walked in and smiled. We all began to embrace each other, lock lips and rub on each other. Tasha kissed my breast while Cassandra kissed me. I lifted Cassandra's blouse and kissed her breast. I enjoyed being with them and at this point, I wanted to leave and have a threesome. We were on our way into one of the stalls, and just then my phone rang.
"Hello."
"Hey Kelley are you coming?"
"Yea, I'm leaving here in about thirty minutes or so."
"Okay. See you in a little while."

I couldn't fight the feeling of wanting to sleep with Tasha and Cassandra. They kissed me and I wanted more. I lodged my body between both and allowed them to have their way with me. I looked at my watch and it was ten o'clock.
"I have to go."
"Where are you going?"
Cassandra placed her hand on the bathroom door when I reached for the handle.
"I was invited to another party."
"I will walk you to your car."
"Okay."
"Bye Tasha and thanks for the drink."
"Bye sexy and you're welcome."
"Can I call you later?"
Cassandra was persistent about seeing me again.
"I will call you."

That call never transpired and I never looked back. But my desire for women was stronger than before. Daniel and I continued to party up North, but as time passed, we stopped going together. I didn't stop hanging up North until I had my son. Daniel never knew. Still to this day he has no idea I was seeing women behind his back. Even if he did know; what could he possibly say when he was sleeping with women behind my back and in front of me. Our relationship started to get stronger, but his mother was just as much as a cock-blocker as he was.

Mama's Boy-3

I started my car, hit 90-94 and drove to Daniel's mothers' house. I exited at ninety-ninth and Halsted, and followed the road around. There were plenty of cars parked outside of her house.

"Hey Kelley, you look good."
"Thank you. So do you."
"Come on in."
"Hello everybody."
"Mama's back here."
"Hi Ms. Harris."
"Hi Kelley."
"Where are you just coming from?"
"I was at a friend's party downtown."
"That's nice."
"Kelley, do you want something to drink?"
"Yep."
"I hope Grace don't pop her ass up over here."
"Why do you say that?"
"I had a talk with her and she refuses to let go."
"I'm leaving if she does."
"We won't be here long."

We listened to blues and oldies, but goodies. I actually had fun at Ms. Harris's house. Daniel and I stepped, but he didn't know what he was doing. We all danced and by the time I looked up it was almost one o'clock in the morning. I felt so much better knowing Daniel wasn't with Grace. I was able to bring the New Year in with him. I would have preferred to do it without the company of his mother, but I took what I could get.

January 2000

I went to Chicago State University (CSU) to register and was kind of intimidated by the idea of attending a four-year university. Attending college was not something anyone in my family experienced so I had no one to encourage me. Daddy always told me to go to school to become an RN, but he never told me about the hard work it took. No one ever said it would be hard or easy. No one ever said I could do it. But, I knew I had to get my BS whether it was in nursing or not. I would be the first in my family to get a Bachelor's degree. The last time I applied at CSU, I was eighteen years old and withdrew because I didn't have enough confidence to stay. Part of me was still somewhat afraid I wouldn't do well, so I just avoided it all together. I applied for the Health Information Administration program.

"I'm proud of you Kelley."

"Thanks Daniel."

"So what will you do in this field?

"Management."

"That's good, finally a woman with goals and dreams. We're gonna make some money."

"I'm gonna make some money."

"She needs to take her ass back to school. I even told her I would help her through school. She doesn't have dental insurance and my mother told me she said she wanted to marry me because I have medical benefits. Her two front teeth are jacked up and every time she smiles, she covers her mouth with her hand." *Laughter from Daniel and me.*

I wasn't interested in hearing Daniel talk about Grace. I felt bad about not applying for the nursing program. I wanted to become an RN, but my confidence was very low. Graduating from Malcolm X. College wasn't enough to skyrocket my confidence. The entire time I attended Malcolm X., I never applied myself to the fullest. I struggled through the program.

"I'm done for today so what do you want to do?"

"I have to work today."

"Okay. I will bring some dinner to your job."

"Cool."

I went home and got everything I needed ready for school, made dinner and drove to Daniel's job.
"Hello."
"Hey Daniel I'm outside your job."
"Oh cool. I'm coming out to get you."
"This looks good. What is it?"
"It's Pink Salmon and Mostaccioli."
"And it tastes damn good."
"Her ass can't even cook. All she knows how to cook is canned spaghetti and meatballs and then she adds cheese."
Daniel laughed, but I didn't find it funny at all. I became very irritated with him talking about Grace. More than often she was the topic of our conversation. He never had anything good to say about her. Daniel had been with Grace for over eleven years and I know there was something about her he appreciated. He behaved as if Grace was the worst person on earth. Time passed and instead of going home to go to sleep, I nodded out in my car.

"I looked up startled and rubbed my eyes."
Daniel knocked on my window.
"Hey baby. I'm off so we can ride out."
"Okay."
Daniel and I went home and did what we usually do until the sun rose. *I'm going to make him a nice breakfast in the morning.* I thought.
Daniel's phone rang at eight o'clock in the morning.
"Hey Ma. Yea. I will be over in about an hour."
"What did your mother want?"
I rolled my eyes and turned over.
"She needs me to take her to the store and then fix her stove."
"Hmmph."
*What the f*ck is wrong with her and his ass? They run to each other like they're f*cking. I ain't never seen a grown ass man run to his mother for every damn thing. He acts like he can't tell her fat ass no.* I thought.
"Kelley I'm getting in the shower. Are you getting in?"
"After I awake, we just went to sleep about an hour ago."
"Why don't you lie back down?"

"I will be back. Let me just take care of my Mama."
"Why do you have to always run over there when she calls? I can see if it's an emergency."
"That's my Mama and she needs me."
"What about me?"
"My mother comes first."
"Wow."
"Look Kelley. You can come with me if you want to."
"I'm going back to sleep. Bye."

Daniel left and ran to his mother as he did from day one. I believed what other people told me about Ms. Harris; she didn't want anyone dating Daniel. She was very controlling and it didn't matter what she did, Daniel always thought she was perfect. She eventually showed me her true colors and it didn't matter, Daniel never believed me. For seven years, I dealt with her manipulative behavior, insults and lies, and her son was just like her. She may have fooled her Daniel, but she didn't fool me.

March 2000
"I don't know why my sons waste their ten cents on you women. They can have whoever they want."

Fat jealous b*tch. Your fat ass is mad because your man ain't sh*t. Quit acting like your son is your man. Sick ass woman. I thought.

I looked at her like she was crazy, but never spoke a word. I stopped by Ms. Harris's house at the request of Daniel. He was on his way there and asked if I would wait. Ms. Harris and I talked and I realized she was a no good, phony, fat, manipulative ass woman. She pretended she was nice and always showed Daniel a side of her that was like Dr. Jeckel. But, I got to see Ms. Hyde more than I bargained for.
"Hey Ma."
Daniel walked in.
"Hey Kelley."

Daniel kissed me and Ms. Harris didn't like that.
"Y'all stop all that. Don't nobody wanna see that."
I laughed sarcastically because I knew she was jealous. She acted like she was f*cking her son.
"Y'all want something to eat?"
"Yea I'm hungry, Ma. Kelley you want some?"
"No. I'm not hungry."
The sh*t is probably nasty. I am ready to leave this damn house. I am not feeling this woman. I thought.
"I have to tell you something when we leave."
"What's wrong?"
"I will tell you when we leave. I could've cooked you some food at home. I'm ready to go."
"Okay. Let me finish and we can go."
Daniel finished his chili and I washed the dishes.
"Aren't you going to add bleach to the dish water?"
Ms. Harris was one of those old school women who still practiced old remedies.
"For what?"
I rinsed out her black cast iron skillet and placed it in the dish rack.
"To kill the germs."
"The dishwashing liquid will do that."
"I always use bleach in my dish water."
"I don't."
Shut the f*ck up talking to me, old backwoods ass lady. It doesn't take a rocket scientist to know that you don't need bleach to clean dishes. Who the hell wants to use bleach on something they have to eat out of? I thought. I finished the dishes and walked towards the living room.
"Ma I will talk to you later."
"Where y'all going?"
"Over Kelley's house."
"What are y'all gonna do over there?"
"Hang out."
"Okay. See y'all later."

B*tch you won't see me later. I thought. I never had enough courage to tell that woman what I wanted to. I allowed her and Daniel to disrespect me. Daniel made me feel as though it didn't matter what his mother did, she was always right. I was in a no-win situation with him and his mother. When she wasn't stressing me out, Grace was stalking or harassing me.

"Now what's wrong Kelley?"
"While I was waiting for you, your mother told me and I quote. *I don't know why my sons waste their ten cents on you women. They can have whoever they want.*
"My mother didn't say that."
"I have no reason to lie."
"She was probably just playing."
"I don't see anything playful about that. That's just disrespectful as hell and she has no right to tell me some sh*t like that. I am your woman."
"I don't think she meant it like that."
"How else did she mean it?"
"You are taking that way out of proportion."
"You need to talk with her and tell her to watch her mouth."
"I'm not saying nothing to my mother. She can say whatever she wants."
"Even if she's wrong, that's f*cked up."
"Before you mess this day up, let's stop talking about my mother."
"Are you going to say something to her?"
"I will talk to her."
"Good."

With her jealous fat ass. She wants him all to herself and doesn't want anyone to have him. Sick b*tch acts like she's f*cking her own son and he runs to her like he's her man. I have never seen mothers invite their grown ass sons out for drinks while her man is present. Hell, I don't even know any men that do that sh*t on a regular. I can see once in a blue moon, but all the time. Their asses need therapy. I thought.

Kelley Porter

April 2000

I found myself in another relationship where I felt like I needed love, and would do anything for it. I was stronger than before, but I wasn't as connected with myself as I thought. Prior to Daniel, I went to church on a regular and stayed focused. This past year became all about Daniel and wanting him to love me. He hurt me in the worst ways. Something wasn't right about my body odor, so I went to see my doctor.

"Hi Dr. Watson."
"How are you Ms. Porter."
"I hope I'm fine."
"What's the problem?"
"I have this odor after taking a shower and it smells like fish."
"Okay. Let me take a look."

Dr. Watson left the room for a few minutes. *I hope this nigga ain't gave me a damn disease. I know something ain't right. I have never smelled like this.* I thought.
"Ms. Porter it looks like you have Trichomonas."
"What is that?"
"It's a sexually transmitted disease."
"I've never had that." I cried.
"Are you sleeping with anyone other than your boyfriend?"
"No. He's the only person I'm sleeping with."
"Well, Kelley you might want to start using condoms."
"I didn't think I had to."
"I'm going to give you a prescription, and I'm sorry you had to experience this. You take care of yourself. Take your time coming out."
"Thank you Dr. Watson."
I was so hurt. I stayed in the patient's room for another five minutes and cried. I knew I hadn't been with anyone else and I assumed Daniel caught the disease from Grace. I never even entertained the thought of him sleeping with other women or behind my back.

My phone rang.
"Hey Kelley."

"Hey."
"What's wrong?"
I answered the phone with sadness in my voice.
"I just left my doctor's office and I have an STD."
"Really, what did he say?"
"Dr. Watson said I have Trichomonas."
"What is that?"
"A sexually transmitted disease. I heard of when I was in school for Medical Technology, but I aint never had it."
"Where are you now?
"I'm on my way to Walgreen."
"I will meet you there."
"Okay."
I was very hurt, but for whatever reason; maybe reality, I wasn't angry at Daniel. I knew he had a woman, so the only person I could be mad at, was me. I should have used a condom and chose not to so that was my fault. I knew he caught the disease from Grace. The way he degraded her made me think she was nothing but a slut. I was way off and was not expecting to hear what I did.
"Hey Kelley."
Daniel startled me as he walked in behind me in the Pharmacy department of Walgreen.
"Hey. Daniel I haven't been with any other men. Did Grace give you this?"
"I don't know."
"Have you slept with someone else?"
"I was with another woman about two weeks ago."
"So you're sleeping with women outside of me and Grace, and without a condom. I can't even be mad at you. I should've known better and used a condom."
"You need to go see a doctor and get some medicine."
"How long do you have to take the medicine?"
"For a week, twice a day for one week."
"I'm sorry Kelley."

We left Walgreen and I went home. Before I could get comfortable and process the information, my phone rang.

"Hello."
"Hey Kelley."
"What the hell do you want?"
"Daniel told me you have an STD."
"He probably got it from your ass."
"I don't have anything."
"Get the f*ck out of here. You're still f*cking him so you have it too."
"I haven't slept with Daniel in a month."
"And you want me to believe that sh*t."
"I really don't care what you believe, but I don't have anything sweetheart."
"You must think I'm a damn fool."
Grace hung the phone up and I was livid. *This b*tch must think I'm stupid. All of a sudden she's not f*cking him when he has a damn disease. I'm not stupid. Her ass has the sh*t too. Lying b*tch.* I thought.

May 2000

Daniel wanted a building. He said he never wanted to buy a house and the reason he did was because his mother suggested it. He thought about asking his mother to help him buy a building and I was so sick of him asking her for anything. I offered to help as long as I made a profit off the building or moved into one of the apartments. I decided I would stay where I was and just help him. The mortgage company approved my loan application and Daniel was excited; he would finally have a building.
"Hey Kelley."
"Hey Daniel. I'm going to sign the paperwork for the home loan today. Have you been looking?"
"Yea, but I haven't found anything yet."
"Why do you have that turtle neck on and it's nice outside."
"I worked on my car."
"Okay. I'm about to take a shower. Do you want to get in with me?"
"Naw, I'm good."
"What? Stop playing Daniel."

"We haven't been with each other in weeks. You better take those clothes off and get in here."
"Alright."
"Is that a passion mark?"
"Where?"
"On your damn neck."
"Yea. Grace did that on purpose. I didn't sleep with her."
"You must think I'm a damn fool."
"Get the f*ck out of my house. Lying bastard! I'm not doing sh*t for you. Ask Grace to help your ass or better yet, do what you do best, and ask your mother."

June 2000
Summer was fierce and so was the amount of pain and drama I experienced. Two months passed and my period hadn't started. I did a urine pregnancy test on myself and it was positive. I didn't know how to feel as I didn't want any kids at that time. I was twenty-eight, in school and still having fun. I called Daniel.

"Hello."
"Hey Daniel, Are you at your mom's place?"
"Yea why?"
"I'm about to stop over there. It's not busy at work and the supervisor suggested someone go home early, so I took the offer."
"Cool."
When I pulled up to Ms. Harris's house, Daniel and his brother were playing catch with a football.
"Hey. What's up?"
"I'm pregnant Daniel."
"Are you serious? How do you know?"
"I just did the test at work. I haven't had a period in two months."
"What are you going to do?"
"I don't want any kids now so I'm going to abort it."
"Okay. I will pay for it so schedule the appointment."

"What are you doing for the rest of the day? It's so nice out here."
"I will probably hang out over here for a little longer."
"Okay. I'm going home. I have homework."
"I will stop by later."
I do not want any kids now. I am still young and traveling. I'm not having this baby. He doesn't want any more kids anyway. Damn.
I have never been pregnant and I'm going to abort my first child. I thought.

****

My doorbell rang.
"Hey Kelley, do you have an appointment?
"Yea, it's Wednesday."
"Okay. I will pay for it and take you down there."
"What's wrong?"
"This is my first time being pregnant."
"Really, you have never been pregnant."
"No. I was on pills for the last ten years and the only reason I stopped taking them is because Dr. Watson suggested I give my body a break."
"Wow. So I'm the first man to get you pregnant?"
"Yep."
"Does anyone else know you're pregnant?"
"My sisters and my friend at work."
"I'm gonna jump in the shower. I'm dirty from throwing that football back and forth"
"That's fine."

Wednesday arrived and we went to Planned Parenthood on the North side of Chicago. There were at least thirty women there and it felt better to know I wasn't alone. Women entered and exited the elevator. This place was cold and emotion-less. No one said a word. We all just kind of glanced at each other and looked away. One name called after another, and then mine. I followed the nurse to an office that felt so small. There was a brown desk that held several pamphlets about abortions and STD's. A large plant sat in the corner behind the desk, and I sat in the chair directly in front of the desk.

"Kelley I'm going to ask you a series of questions."
"Okay."
"Is this your choice?"
"Yes."
"Do you want to abort your child?"
"Yes."
"Have you ever been pregnant before?"
"No."
"So this is your first time being pregnant?"
"Yes."
"Okay. The procedure doesn't take long, but it also depends on whether you are asleep or awake. The prices also vary."
"Do you want to be…Are you okay?
"No."
"What's wrong?"
"I can't do it. I can't do it. I don't want to kill my baby. This isn't right. No. I can't do it."
I fell to the floor and cried.
"Ms. Porter, you are not ready and we will not do the procedure on you. If you want to reschedule you can, but you have one month left before it's too late."
She exited the office and came back in with Daniel.
"I can't do it. I'm not ready."
I cried and shook my head from left to right.
"If you can't do it Kelley, let's leave."
"Okay."

I walked out to the waiting room and it seemed as if everyone stared at me. I dropped my head in shame. On the ride home, I was completely silent. Daniel looked over at me a few times and grabbed my hand. I cried as I looked out the window. *I thought I could do it. This is my first time being pregnant. I didn't plan this baby. He doesn't want any more kids. I can't have a baby now. I really don't know what to do. I'm in school. I started a new career.* I thought.

"I will call you later."

I got out of Daniel's car and went in the house. He wanted me to have an abortion, but he didn't use a condom. He constantly shared with me how he didn't want any more kids, and although I was uncertain about having children, the entire process of aborting my first child saddened me. A week later, we went back to Planned Parenthood and sat in the same quiet, and emotionless waiting room. The only noise I heard was the telephone ring, the elevator doors open, and patients' names called.

"Kelley Porter."

"Right here."

"Come with me please."

We went into one of the patient's room and the nurse took my blood pressure. This room was lifeless.

"Your blood pressure is normal, so I will take you over to the see the doctor."

"Okay."

I tried to stay calm. I didn't want them to send me home again so I controlled my emotions. On the inside, I was very scared and in pain. We walked down a short hall, and entered another lifeless room. There was a bed with a bright light over it attached to the ceiling; a blood pressure monitor, a desk that held a computer and a chair. Everything was so pale.

"Hi Ms. Porter."

"Hi."

"Is this your first pregnancy?"

"Yes."

"Why do you want to have an abortion?"

"I'm not ready for kids."

"Did my nurse explain the procedure to you?

"Yes."
"And you prefer to have the procedure done asleep."
"Yes."
"Okay. I will start an IV sedation and you will be asleep in a few minutes."
"How long does this take?"
"Not long at all, maybe about twenty minutes."
I felt groggy and don't remember anything after the doctor said twenty minutes. I awoke in another room and rubbed my stomach. There was a maxi pad already attached to my underwear.
"How are you feeling?"
One of the nurses stood over my bed.
"Cramping, but I'm okay."
"Good. Here are your discharge papers so you can get dressed, go home and get some rest."
"Thank you."
I felt somewhat relieved. More than half of me did not want any kids. I wasn't ready. I enjoyed my life and didn't want a baby stopping me. I dressed and entered the elevator that led to the path of hell. The elevator opened and everyone stared at me like I was a murderer and indeed I was. I killed my child. I had no idea what aborting my first child would lead to. Daniel held me as we walked to the car. The entire ride home was so painful.
"How do you feel Kelley?"
"My stomach hurts. I'm cramping really bad. Please watch the bumps in the road."
I began to cry.
"Okay. I will be careful. Do you want me to come by your place with you for a while?"
"No. Just take me to fill this prescription and drop me off. I need some sleep."
"Okay."
I had nothing else to say. I sat quietly and cried to myself. We made it to my place and Daniel walked me up the stairs and helped me get into bed.
"Kelley, I will call to check on you later."

"Okay."
I looked at the ceiling, and unable to control my tears, I cried like a baby. I was hurt and began to feel depressed. The shame was killing me. I wept like a baby. My eyes were red and puffy. More days than expected, were tearful, puffy eyes, call offs, alcohol and sadness. I had the next few days off work, but I had school. A week passed after the abortion and I visited Daniel. I didn't like his mother at all. As a matter of fact, I wished death on her.
"Hey Ms. Harris."
"Hi Kelley. How are you?"
"I'm fine. I had the abortion."
"Stop telling all your business."
"It's not like Daniel wasn't going to tell you."
"It's your business."
"I just thought I'd share it with you."
"That's fine, but don't tell so many people."
"My family, you and Daniel are the only people who know."
"Oh. Okay."
*What the f*ck is wrong with this b*tch. She knows damn well she know already and wanna act like Daniel didn't tell her. Fat ass.* I thought.
"Kelley are you ready?"
"Yea."
"Where y'all going?"
"We're going out Ma."
"Okay."
"Why does she always have to know where we're going?"
"That's just how Mama is."
"She is nosey and controlling."
"Watch your mouth before you ruin our day."
"I've just never heard of anybody's mother always calling one son out of the six she has on a regular, asking where you're going, wanting to party, and go to the riverboat. That's what your woman would do?
"That's just Mama."
"Hmmph."

I silenced myself because I realized Daniel's mother was more important to him than anyone in this world. To speak ill of her was grounds for an argument. Eventually I stopped caring and gave Daniel a mouthful about his mother and him.
"I want a baby."
"Are you serious?"
"Yes. So if you don't want any more kids, I suggest you use a condom because if I get pregnant again, I'm keeping my baby."
"Girl, stop playing. Do you really want a child?"
"Yea, I will be thirty in a year and I want a baby. So use a condom from here on out or you are going to have three babies."
"You mean four."
"Four?"
"I have an older daughter, but I don't see her. Her mother called me after six months and said she was pregnant, and then put me on child support after she had her. I don't even know if the kid is mine."
"Did you test him?"
"Nope."
"Why not?"
"I just said f*ck this sh*t."
"How old is she?"
"She's a few years older than my other daughter."
"Wow."
"They pay this b*tch almost a thousand dollars a month."
"Damn."
"I can't afford any more kids. Then you know I have a small son and he's only two."
"Do you see him?"
"Not really."
"Why? That's your child."
"I don't give a f*ck."
"Daniel, don't be like that. You need to spend time with your son. "Besides, I'd like to meet him."
"Yeah, one day."

We went up North to party and the next morning his mother called. I was so tired of him running to her so I snapped.
"Hey Ma."
"What the f*ck does she want?"
"Okay. I will be there in a minute."
"What the f*ck? Do you always run she calls?"
"I told your ass that is my Mama and you need to shut the f*ck up."
"Take your Mama's boy ass on. As a matter of fact, tell your Mama to f*ck you and suck your d*ck. Tell her fat ass to cook your food, and do the sh*t I do. What the f*ck is wrong with you? Tell her to wash your damn clothes; oh I forgot she does? Sad ass."
"Watch your motherf*cking mouth."
"No. F*ck this sh*t. I'm sick of her fat ass calling every time we're together and you run like a little boy. The doctors cut f*cking cord over thirty years ago, now act like a damn man."
"F*ck you. Stupid ass."
"No you're the stupid ass. Running to your mother like a b*tch. Five other boys and you're the only one she calls. Her ass don't want anyone to have you. She knows what the f*ck she's doing and she has a man. You're so damn dumb you don't see what she's doing. She is your damn demise."

"Shut the f*ck up Kelley."
"You shut the f*ck up and get out. Stupid ass."
"That's my Mama and you better watch your damn mouth b*tch"
"Your mother is a b*tch and I'm sick of this sh*t; you, your mother and Grace. So until you are ready to make your mind up as to who you want, you are free to do whatever you want and so am I. I will not bother you anymore. You can leave."

I slammed the door. *He is the dumbest motherf*cker on earth. He acts like he's f*cking his mother. Ain't nobody got time for this sh*t. Both of their asses are mentally unstable. That is one sick ass relationship. I deserve better than this sh*t.* I thought.

July 2000

Some time passed before I saw Daniel again. I was sick and tired of dealing with his mess. I loved and missed Daniel, but I just couldn't bare all the pain. There were too many days of tears, not wanting to eat, disruption at work, lies, betrayal and deceit. I had enough.

My phone rang.
"Hello."
"Hey Kelley, how are you doing?"
"I'm fine and you?"
"I've been okay. I miss you."
"I miss you too."
"Can I come by?"
"Why?"
"So we can talk."
"That's fine."
Daniel came by and I didn't expect this outcome.
"I want you back."
"Daniel you're not ready. You're still running the streets and sleeping around. We can just be friends."
"I can't be your friend. I'm not dating Grace anymore and I will do better with my mother."
"Really."
"I love you and if I didn't have so much baggage, I would marry you. So can we try again?"
"As long as you're not lying to me."
"Do you wanna go shoot some pool with me?"
"Sure. Let's go right up the street to Bills."
"Can I see your phone so I can call Nicki?"
"Sure."
The phone rang.
"Hello."
"Hey Nicki."
"Hey Kelley."
"Do you wanna meet me and Daniel…. Hold on Nicki."
"Hello."
"Hi, may I speak to Daniel?"
There was another woman on Daniel's other line.

"Do you mind calling back in a few minutes?"
I wasn't too concerned about that call because I knew Daniel had female friends that he wasn't sleeping with.
"Hello Nicki, sorry about that. Hold on Nicki."
"Hello."
"May I speak to Daniel?"
Whoever this woman was, she was persistent.
"Hold on."
"Answer your phone. Some woman keeps calling."

Hello.
Hey Daniel, I thought you said we were going to see each other tonight.
Tell your sister, I will call her tomorrow about fixing her car.
What? Are we going to see each other?

"Who is that? I know damn well you did not just ask to get back with me and now this bullsh*t."
I smacked Daniel's phone out of his hand.
"What are you talking about? That's a girl from my job and I worked on her sister's car."
"I heard the whole f*cking conversation. I heard her talking. You know what, let me out this car you stupid bastard. Tired, dog ass motherf*cker. You could have left me the f*ck alone. I wasn't bothering you. I gave your ass a free pass to do whatever the hell you wanted. I asked you to leave me out of this sh*t. If you want to f*ck women, go ahead, but leave me the f*ck alone."

I opened the door, took my keys and scratched the paint right off his car. He threw my purse out and I jumped on the hood of his car and held on as he drove through the lot. I keyed the hood of his car and then he stopped. I got off and walked home.

*If this b*tch think this sh*t is over he's got another thing coming. I'm going to get his ass. He could have left me the f*ck alone. Begging me to get back with his ass and still f*cking other women. I'll show his ass.*

I thought. I called Daniel's phone and left several messages about him hitting me, but he never hit me. I drove to his house and called the police from the pay phone.

"Nine one one where's your emergency?"
"My boyfriend just slapped me and I want him arrested."
"Where is he now?"
"At his house."
"Where are you?"
"I'm at a pay phone down the street from his house."
"Stay there and I will send an officer."
Sirens sounded and I patiently waited for the officer to park. We drove to Daniel's house and they knocked on his door. He looked out the window and refused to open the door.
"Sir, if you don't open the door, we will kick it in."
"Kick my door in for what? I didn't do sh*t."
"This young woman has filed a complaint against you for slapping her."
"I ain't touched her ass."
"Yes, you did. You lying bastard. That ain't the first time. Every time he gets angry or caught cheating, he blames the sh*t on me and then hits me."
I cried.
"She is f*cking lying. Listen to the voice messages on my phone."
The officer listened to the messages I left on Daniel's phone, and was convinced I was telling the truth.
"Put your hands behind your back, sir."
"I didn't do sh*t. She is f*cking lying."
"She said in the voicemail you were not going to get away with hitting her this time. Now put your hands behind your back before this gets ugly."
"This is some bullsh*t. I need to get my son."
I didn't know Daniel had his son with him so I had to change things. I didn't want his baby taken away.
"Follow us to the station to Ms. Porter."
"Okay."

The police officer filed some paperwork and before I signed, Daniel and I had words.

"You're foul as hell for this sh*t. You know damn well I didn't hit you."

"Yes, you did. You damn liar."

"It's a damn Sunday afternoon and I don't want to be bothered with this sh*t.

The police officer interrupted.

"If you let me hit him back we can leave."

"I'm not looking."

The police officer turned his head and I slapped Daniel so hard I busted his eardrum. I wanted to bust his damn head. I didn't believe in violence, but I was extremely angry.

"Now get the hell out of my station."

"How am I going to get home with my son?"

"I'll drop you off."

I offered to take Daniel home, but he wasn't interested.

"Naw."

"I will take you back, just don't ruin my damn Sunday with this mess."

I went home and although that felt good, it also felt horrible. Daniel came by the next day and told me how he felt. He didn't want to date me anymore. I was sad, yet confused at the same time. I broke up with him and now he was trying to dump me. Daniel left and we didn't see each other for some time. I cried for days because I knew I was wrong and I missed Daniel. I called him for weeks and he never responded.

My phone rang.

"Hello."

"Hey Kelley."

"B*tch what do you want?"

"I hope you don't think you can befriend Daniel and think that sh*t was okay. You thought you were better than me. You're mirror image."

"No b*tch you wish you were like me."

"He told me about how you keyed his car up."

"So f*cking what. Now stop calling and harassing me b*tch before
I file harassment charges against your silly ass."
I hung the phone up. Grace decided to call me after Daniel ran and told her what happened. *No this motherf*cker didn't tell her. Ole punk ass nigga. He acts just like a b*tch. Always running and telling some sh*t. That motherf*cker will miss me because I'm going to ignore his raggedy ass when he call.* I thought.

August 2000
"Hey Mama, how are you feeling? Hey Lionel."
"Hey baby. I'm tired and not feeling too well. This new medicine they have me on is wearing me down."
"Is that the experimental drug for Hepatitis?"
"Yes."
"The side effects are pretty heavy, but you will be okay. When is your next appointment?"
"I don't do back for two weeks and then they will do another liver biopsy on me."
"Okay. Do you want me to take you?"
"Yes."
"When you feel a little better Mama, we're going to go out and dance."
"I need to get out."
"You will real soon. I'm about to meet with Daniel. We're going out to eat."
"Okay."
"I love you Mama."
"I love you too baby."
"Bye Lionel. I love you."
"I love you too Kelley. Bye."

****

Daniel and I went to a Chinese restaurant in Calumet Park and I expressed my interest in having a baby.

"I know you don't want any more kids, but that abortion really messed me up. I think about that day, every day. I think about what she or he would've looked like, buying clothes, feeding and playing with him or her."

"Kelley I don't want any more kids. I can't even take care of the ones I have."

"We're still having sex without a condom and when we do, I pray I miss my period."

"You have got to be kidding me."

"Nope. I'm dead serious. I want a baby by you."

Daniel's phone rang.

"Hey Ma, okay. Give me thirty minutes."

"Are you kidding me?"

"Don't start no sh*t with me."

"You know what; I'm not. Just take me the hell home."

I slammed the car door, exited and didn't look back.

My phone rang.

"What?!"

"Kelley you need to quit tripping about my Mama needing me."

"Y'all act like y'all boyfriend and girlfriend. That sh*t ain't even normal. Then you criticize her boyfriend like you're jealous."

"That nigga is broke and he's an alcoholic. He doesn't need to live there."

"Why the hell are you so worried about your Mama and her man? She's a grown ass woman. If she didn't want him there, I'm sure he wouldn't be there."

"Naw. My Mama too nice. That nigga don't have anywhere to stay."

"Daniel don't be a damn fool. Your mother is using your ass as her man because she knows you will do anything for her. I told you she was your demise. No woman is going to marry you and you will be lonely for a long time."

"I don't give a f*ck about marrying a damn woman."

"You're saying that sh*t now. But when your Mama is dead and gone, what are you going to do? She takes care of you like she's your woman. I don't have time for this sh*t. Leave me the f*ck alone!"

I hung the phone up.

"What Daniel?!"

"I'm sorry. It's just that I love my momma, and when she needs me, I need to be there."

"I understand that, but for every f*cking thing. She calls you in the morning and we could've just finished f*cking and you go running. It's obvious you don't give a sh*t about me. So how about just leave me the f*ck alone.

"I do care about you Kelley. Sh*t, I have a lot going on. Grace is stressing me the hell out and now you're adding to it."

"Not any more tonight. Bye."

Daniel called back trying to apologize for dismissing me for his mother, but I knew it wouldn't change. He was a Mama's boy who was controlled and manipulated by his mother years before I even met him. There was no help for him. His mother already ruined his life. A few days later, Daniel called me while I was at work. I really wasn't interested in talking to him. But I found out it wasn't him who wanted to talk.

"Chemistry, this is Kelley, how can I help you?"
"Hey Kelley."
"I'm at work. What do you want?"
"Grace is over here and she wants to talk to you."
"Why does she wanna talk to me?"
"She said she just wants to talk."
"I just bet she does. Why is she at your house?"
"She stopped by to talk so just come by on your lunch."
"Yea sure."

I don't know why this ugly b*tch wants to talk to me. Ain't sh*t to talk about. I thought. My lunch was an hour and Daniel's house was only fifteen minutes away. I decided to take the early dinner instead of later. I arrived at Daniel's house and was face to face again with Grace.

"What's up Daniel? Where is she?"
"Downstairs listening to the music."
"Okay. Call her up here."
"Hi Kelley."
"Hey Grace. What's up?"

"You hurry up and ran over here didn't you?"
"Didn't you say you wanted to talk? I don't have time for this sh*t."
"Daniel and I are getting back together so you need to step back. If you had stayed out in the beginning, we would've never broken up."
"You can't blame me for this sh*t. It takes two. I don't have time for this sh*t."
Daniel stood there and listened to us argue.
"I'm leaving."
Grace opened the door.
"Naw, you don't have to leave."
"If she ain't leaving, then neither am I."
"Get the hell off my couch."
"F*ck this raggedy ass couch and you too."
"Daniel don't want your ass, and I'm not going to stop f*cking him."
"I guess we will both be f*cking him. Now what?"
"Is she going to leave because if not, I am?"
"I have school and work and don't have time for this bullsh*t."
"She thinks she better than me."
"No. You think I'm better than you."
"Go back downstairs Grace."
"If you wanna be with her ass then go ahead, but don't call my damn phone."

I walked out of Daniel's house and drove back to work. *The nerve of both of them b*tches asking me to come and talk only to hear some bullsh*t. I should have never left work for his sorry ass. His raggedy ass better not call my damn phone.* I thought.

It didn't matter what Daniel did or how much pain he caused me, I always forgave him and allowed him back in my life. He treated like garbage. I told myself over and over again to leave and never give him another chance, but I did. I stopped by Ms. Harris's house at the request of Daniel.

"Hi Ms. Harris."

"Hi Kelley."
"Daniel asked me to come over until he gets here."
"Where is he?"
"I have no idea."
"Well come down to the basement with me and help me go through a few things."
"That's fine."
We sat down and began looking through magazines, and other items Ms. Harris wanted to throw out.
"You know I used to have a friend until you came along."
"Who?"
I looked at Ms. Harris waiting for her to respond.
"My son."
"Ma, Kelley, where y'all at!?"
Daniel finally made it and I was glad. I left Ms. Harris in the basement and went upstairs to meet Daniel.
"What's wrong?"
"I'm sick of your mother and I'm going home."
"What happened?"
"It doesn't matter. You're not going to do sh*t anyway. You never do. You're not going to believe me. I'm going home."
Daniel walked behind me and we talked outside for a moment. He sat in his car while I walked over to my car to get my cigarettes. A few minutes later Grace stormed up, walked to Daniel's car and started swinging on him. He tried to defend himself by blocking and grabbing her arms. But she still managed to scratch his face. I stood there and watched her.
"You just don't have no self-esteem."
Grace walked pass me with this angry look on her face. I walked to Daniel's car.
"Sick ass b*tch. I'm sick of her mother*cking ass."
Daniel looked in his rear-view mirror.
"I don't know why you accept that sh*t from her."
"Let's go to your house."
"That's fine."

Grace ripped Daniel's skin off of his cheek. *She's going to hit him one more time and he's going to beat her ass. I wouldn't* *be surprised if he's already done it. Violent ass b*tch.* I thought. Daniel and I made it home and the thought of talking to him about what his mother said to me was not an option. He was already pissed off and I didn't want to add to it. But I was sick of her jealous fat ass talking sh*t to me. Daniel refused to say anything to her and it didn't matter what she did. He always made an excuse or defended her. He always told me his mother can do what she wanted and he wasn't going to say saying anything to her. Daniel and I had a few drinks and watched movies until we went to sleep.

September 2000
I stopped by Daniel's house uninvited and he refused to answer the door, and that pissed me off. I knew he had company, but I wasn't sure who it was. After arguing, I kicked his window out and drove home. I pulled up to my house and before I parked my car, two police officers pulled up, and arrested me. I was in a holding cell for almost ten hours. I called a friend of mine and asked her to bond me out. She agreed. Daniel filed charges against me, but never came to court so the judge dismissed the charges. I hated him and all the pain he caused me. I became a very scorn and angry woman, but somehow I always gave Daniel chance after chance. He never changed, but the love I had for him eventually did. During the Winter break, I visited my friend Anna in Miami Florida.

December 2000
It was about five inches of snow on the ground and I was ready to fly out to Miami, Florida. Daniel dropped me off at the airport and parked my car in front of his house. I made it safely to Miami and Anna picked me up from the airport.
"Hey girl."
"Hey Anna, it's so good to see you."
We hugged.
"Girl we're gonna have some fun, but you know I go to church a lot."

"That's not why I'm here. I'm here to kick it and party."

South Beach is a so beautiful. I strolled along the beach in my two piece thong outfit. I met and conversed with Tyson Bedford. The entire Lakers team was at one of the parties I attended. I danced like there was nobody watching and of course there was; Horace Grant and many of the other NBA players. I saw Shemar Moore and I love that man. I had so much fun. I smoked Cuban cigars and drank Cristal. I hung with the rich Cubans and never had to pay to enter a club. I went to strip clubs and enjoyed the lap dances from the female strippers. My time in Miami was the best and on my last day there, I realized my period hadn't fallen. I still enjoyed my last day with Hennessy and Cuban cigars. I was happy there was a possibility I was finally pregnant again. Anna dropped me off at the airport and Nicki picked me up from Midway. As soon as I got home, I called Dr. Watson scheduled an appointment and the results were in.

Love Child- 4

Six months after my first abortion, it was a pleasure to tell Daniel, I was pregnant again. I shared with him several times I wanted a baby, but he continued to have unprotected sex with me. I guess he thought I was kidding. All he concerned himself with was having three children by three different women. I consciously made a decision to have a baby by him whether he wanted more kids or not, and whether he had a woman. He had full control of simply using a condom and he consciously chose not to.
"Hi Daniel."

"Did you have fun in Miami?"
"I sure did and would love to go back. I met so many great people and never had to pay for anything. But that's not why I called you over. I wanted you to know I'm two months pregnant."
"Okay. Do you want me to take you back to the clinic?"
"No. I'm not having an abortion."
I frowned at Daniel.
"What do you mean?"
"Just what I said; I'm not having an abortion."
"Kelley I don't want any more kids and I sure as hell can't pay for any more."
"I told you I wanted a child and, I told you to use a condom."
"Why didn't you take some pills or some sh*t?"
"You knew I was off pills when I met you. That was my tenth year and Dr. Watson told me to take a break. So don't act like you didn't know. I aborted my first baby and told you if I got pregnant again, I was keeping my baby."
"This is f*cked up."
"Maybe for you. I could easily tell my baby you're dead."
"I don't want any more f*cking kids."
"Too bad because the only thing I'm going to abort is you."
I opened my front door.
Daniel glared at me as he walked out the door. I was completely done with him and there was no way I was going to allow him or Grace to stress me out during my pregnancy

About an hour after Daniel left, my phone rang.
"Hello."
"So you're pregnant Kelley?"
"Yep, and I'm so happy."
"I don't want you to have Daniel's baby!"
"Too bad b*tch because I am and please don't call my phone any more. I don't need the stress."
I hung the phone up in Grace's face and called Daniel. I told him to leave me alone and to tell Grace to leave me alone. I wanted nothing to do with him or her. I refrained from having sex with him. He called from time to time and accompanied me to some of my doctors' visits. For the most part, I tried to stay away from him.

March 2001

I was five months pregnant and feeling somewhat sad about my relationship with Daniel. He was there for me as much as he could be, but his stress level was enormous and Grace was still very much a part of his life. I still loved Daniel, but, not more than I loved my baby. If having my child meant losing Daniel then so be it. I wanted my baby and neither Daniel nor Grace would stop me from having it. I know both of them did things to hurt me intentionally, but it didn't matter. I got the best part of Daniel. Shemar was no mistake and he was a love child on my part. One day at work I decided to call Daniel.

"Hello. Hello. Hello."
I could hear the sounds of moaning and groaning so I hung the phone up. I called back, and the same thing; moaning and groaning. I'm not sure if Daniel was sexing Grace, or if she was doing that on purpose to hurt me. Either way, it hurt me. I took my lunch, drove to Daniel's house and knocked on the door.
"Yea, what's up Kelley?"
"I just called your phone and heard you sexing someone. I heard a woman moaning. Who do you have in there? Are you sleeping with Peggy, or is Grace in there?"
"I don't have anyone in my house."

"Well, can I use the bathroom?"
"Naw."
"Why can't I use the bathroom if you don't have company?"
"Kelley, I don't have time for this shit."
Peggy was Daniel's roommate after Tracey filed Child Support. Tracey was Daniel's youngest son's mother. I tried to force my way in and we wrestled in front of his house.
"You ain't sh*t. I know someone is in there."
"What's the problem over there?"
Someone called the police.
"I stopped by my boyfriend's house and because he has a b*tch in there, he won't let me use the bathroom and then he shoved me."
"She's a damn lie. She tried to force her way into my house and I don't want her in here."
"If she's your girlfriend, why won't you let her in?"
"I don't have time for this shit and she needs to leave."
"Are you pregnant?"
"Five months."
"You better be careful before I arrest you for putting your hands on pregnant woman."
"You go ahead and leave. Don't stay where you're not wanted."
"Thank you and I'm leaving now."

I drove back to work crying and called Daniel's phone at least twenty-five times, and left vulgar messages. I was so hurt and pissed off. After the police appeared, I knew for certain Grace was in his house. She called the police. I wanted to hurt both of them. I wanted to cause them the same pain they caused me. I began to regret having anything to do with Daniel.

April 2001
I was six months pregnant and feeling pretty good. I had mixed emotions about Daniel being around me because I didn't want him to cause me and my baby any stress. I cried many days because of his absence, but I held my head high for my baby's sake. Daniel was mad at me because I chose to keep my child. I visited him and he was in the garage doing a

few things. He appeared happy to see me. He hugged me and rubbed my stomach. We chatted for a bit and on my way to my car, Grace pulled up.
"I will see you later, Daniel."
"Hey Kelley."
Grace approached me as I walked to my car.
"Grace, what are you doing?!"
Daniel walked in our direction.
"She needs to get the hell out of my face."
"I ought to beat your ass."
"Yeah, go ahead and hit me and your ass will go to jail for assaulting a pregnant woman. Stupid ass."
Grace walked away from me and I got in my car, blew the horn, and pulled off.

July 2001
"Daniel, can I have my baby shower in your basement?"
"Sure, that's fine."
Daniel seemed a little off these days. I know he was upset about me being pregnant, but he wasn't putting much more energy into my pregnancy. Something else was bothering him.
"Kelley, Grace will move back in after you have your baby shower."
"Why would you let her move back in?"
"I had to put my roommate out and now I can't afford to pay for this house now. I did everything I could do for my son and that b*tch filed child support, and now she's getting over eight hundred dollars a month."
"That is messed up, but you didn't start keeping your son until I convinced you to, and he was almost two years old. I'm sure that pissed her off."
"That don't f*cking matter."
"Yes it does and then you allowed Grace to stop you from having your son over there. Daniel, did you forget you told me she didn't want the baby around. You should never allow a woman to interfere in your relationship with your child. And you're letting her move back in. So what do you think she's going to do now? Although you didn't want any more kids, I

need you to bond with your son. The first year is very important and you better not allow that b*tch to interfere. I don't want your money. All I want is for you to father your son. Don't make the same mistakes Daniel."
"She's not going to interfere with sh*t. The only reason she's moving back in, is because I need help."
"That's on you. I don't have to deal with her unstable ass. You shouldn't either. But do what you have to do."
"She's moving back in on Monday."
"That's your sh*t. I have classes on Tuesday and Thursday from nine o'clock until three o'clock. I'm finally in the program so classes will be a lot longer."
"That's fine. We will talk more after the baby is born."
Grace moved back in and I called his phone on purpose at one o'clock in the morning, or when I felt like. I really didn't give a sh*t about hurting her or him. All that mess I had to deal with; it was now her turn. I wanted to wreak havoc on them so they would be miserable just like I was, and it worked.

August 2001
I began to have cramps that wouldn't stop. Dr. Watson told me if the cramps were five minutes apart, I was in labor. It was about ten o'clock at night and I drove to Daniel's house. Grace answered the door.
"What do you want Kelley?"
"Go tell Daniel I'm in labor and he needs to take me to the hospital."
Daniel immediately came out and took me Trinity hospital. He left and came back. Mama was in the room with me and so was Daniel. Allen, Chrissy, Nicki and the rest of my family were in the waiting room. I received two injections of epidural because the pain was excruciating, and directly after the anesthesiologist administered the second one, I went from two centimeters of dilation to ten. I pressed the nurse's button and told her I was wet down below. I could hear the overhead page calling Dr. Watson. He finally walked in my room.

"Alright Kelley, let's get this baby out of you. Kelley, when I tell you to push, I need you to push as hard as you can."

"Okay."
"Push Kelley."
I pushed and pushed.
"Push Kelley Push!"
I pushed and pushed and pushed. My son's head exposed, but that wasn't enough.
"Kelley we need to get this baby out of you now! Push Kelley push, push down like you're having a bowel movement! Push as hard as you can!"
"I am. I am."
I was weak and exhausted. I felt a sense of relief, but I didn't hear my baby. I laid there waiting, exhausted with a dry mouth. Moments later, my little blessing screamed. I smiled.
"Is he cute? Is he okay?"
"Yes Kelley. Your son is okay. We will bring him to you in one minute. I will go get your family."
"Here is your baby Kelley. Do you have a name for him?"
"Shemar, like Shemar Moore."

I cried as I looked at my son. He was the most beautiful baby I'd ever seen. He was born at five-forty six in the morning, twenty-one inches long, and six pounds, four ounces. His skin was so wrinkled. He was very light-skinned, almost white with blue eyes and with a peanut shaped head. I kissed Shemar and told him I love him. I wanted Shemar as he was no mistake. I wanted him with every fiber of my being, and nothing and no one was going to hurt my baby. Daniel signed the birth certificate and held Shemar. He kissed him and stayed for a while. After everyone left, the nurse came in to check on us.

"Hi Ms. Porter, how are you feeling?"
"I'm okay, just tired."
"It's time for your baby's feeding, bottle or breast?"
"Breast."
"Okay. Do you know how?"
"No."
"Okay. Let me help you."

Shemar fed from my breast and I was totally amazed. I was truly a proud mom.

"Kelley when the doctor yelled at you it was because your baby's heart rate dropped. It was down to fifty-eight. He almost died."
I looked at the nurse in shock and was totally silent.
"But he's going to be fine now. We're going to keep him and you for two more days to make certain. The Neonatologist will be in to see you in the morning."
"Okay. Thank you."

I wept and rubbed Shemar's hair. When he fell asleep, I picked him up and laid him on my chest. I thought about the abortion I had and the thought of losing Shemar made me cry. He was my love child. I loved Daniel and for that reason I wanted a baby by him. I never wanted a child by any man I dated or slept with. Although Daniel was a lying dog, I fell in love with who I thought he was or could be. I wasn't interested in keeping Daniel and I never thought once having Shemar would make him stay. I wanted a child by Daniel and especially after aborting my first child.

Dr. Wharton discharged me the day I was born. How amazing was that? I gave birth to a child born under the same stars as me and two days before my birthday; a little Leo. That was the first time I ever forgot the day I was born. Shemar was the best birthday gift I asked for. Daniel picked me up with the car seat and we took Shemar home. After Daniel dropped me off, he left immediately. I was scared sh*tless home alone with a newborn baby. Mama wanted to help, but I needed the experience.

Shemar always slept right next to me in my bed while I held his hand. Many days I couldn't sleep. I thought Shemar was going to die. I thought I would smother him. I had all these horrible thoughts and doubts in myself about caring for Shemar. I cried all the time and was so afraid to let him sleep in his crib, so he never did. Dr. Watson gave me the confidence and courage I needed to remove my fears and doubts of being a new mom. After that day, I was ready to raise my child. Although I didn't completely walk away from Daniel, keeping my child was the best decision. I thank the Universe I kept my baby because he changed my life.

Karma-5

"Hey Daniel."
"Hey."
"Everything Shemar needs, is in his bag. Please make sure to change and feed him. If he cries, he's wet, sleepy or hungry."
I left and went on about my business. About eight hours later, I went to pick Shemar up.
"Did you feed him?"
"Yeah, I fed him."
"Why the hell is his bottle still full?"
"Man, I don't have time for this sh*t."
"Sorry ass nigga. This is your son. What the f*ck is wrong with you? You're allowing a b*tch to tell you how to treat or be with your kids. Your ass is going to hell. Didn't your other baby mama just file child support because you allowed Grace to stop the baby from coming around? Your ass haven't learned yet."

By the time I picked Shemar up, his bottle was still full, his Similac hadn't been opened and his diaper was wet. His voice was hoarse and that made me think he cried for a long time. I was in an uproar and had to calm myself. I took my baby home, fed and cleaned him. *That bi*ch is going to hell. What type of woman would try to interfere with a man and his child? She is a rotten, sorry ass female. His dumb ass ain't going to ever have sh*t. He needs to put her ass out. Both of their asses are dumb as hell.* I thought.

After that day, Daniel decided to keep Shemar at my place and I was totally okay with that. I never trusted Grace around my child. She didn't like me so why would she like my son. Daniel promised me he wouldn't allow Grace to interfere. His biggest fear was me filing child support if he didn't do right by Shemar. I honestly had no interest in filing. I just wanted him to do right by his son whether he wanted him or not. I put Shemar to sleep and started my homework. My phone rang, and I had a feeling it was Grace.
"Hello."
"Hey Kelley."

"What the hell do you want?"
"I don't want that damn baby around my daughter!"
"Too damn bad, they are brothers and sisters and you need to get over it."
We argued back and forth and I don't think either of us heard what the other said. The harassment, arguing and drama went on for two years. Grace always threatened me, drove by my house or called my phone. I had reason to believe she keyed my car; but I had no proof. She threatened me while I was pregnant and even threatened to kick my ass after I delivered my son. Six months after Shemar was born, she came through on one of her threats.

Daniel came by later that evening to see Shemar. At around ten pm his telephone rang.
"This b*tch just left a message that said she's outside."
"Who?"
"Grace."
Daniel's phone rang.
"Hello. Why the f*ck are you over here?"
"Daniel you need to take that outside. Shemar is asleep. Go deal with her outside. That's your damn problem. I don't want this sh*t around my baby."

Daniel went outside and I decided to call the police. I had enough of her coming to my damn house. I went downstairs to talk to the police, but Grace left already. She poured milk shake all over Daniel's car. I really didn't understand why he remained involved with her. Grace assumed her moving in was going to stop Daniel from being around me and Shemar. She was completely wrong. Daniel put her out of his house again. He realized the mistakes he made in the past and didn't want to repeat them. Daniel fell in love with Shemar.

"What happened?"
"She pulled the damn door off the hinges. I'm sick of her ass."

"I told you not to let her move back in. All she wanted to do was to stop you from seeing me and Shemar. You're gonna learn one day."
"I'm not even going back over there. Her ass got to go."
"I don't want this mess around Shemar and I would appreciate it if you continued to come by here and keep your son. I don't trust her."
"That's cool Kelley. I can get a break from her ass. Not to mention, I love Shemar and I wanna be in his life. He's my son."
Right before Daniel got comfortable, my telephone rang.
"What Grace?"
"The only reason he's being nice to your ass is because he doesn't want you to file child support."
"B*tch stop calling my phone."
"Was that Grace?"
"Yep."
"Let me take my ass home. Kelley, I will talk to you later."
At this time, I really didn't care about Daniel leaving. I had my son and did not want my baby growing up like I did or around any abuse at all. He was growing quickly. Mama became my regular babysitter. She was always at my place and people thought she lived with me.

October 2001
"Daniel, I'm pregnant again and I'm not having it. So I need you to help me pay for an abortion."
"How did that happen?"
"The same way the first two happened."
We drove back to Planned Parenthood again and the same procedure. The only difference was, I did not feel as bad this time around. I did not want more kids at that time.

February 2002
I was back in the gym and feeling great. I went to Bally's on eighty-seventh and Kedzie.
"Hi Kelley."
"B*tch get the f*ck away from me."
"I'm just saying hi to you. You're lucky I don't beat your ass."

"Yeah. Whatever."

Grace walked away and into the locker room. I finished my run on the treadmill and spoke with one the managers about her harassing me. I walked in the locker room and tried to talk with Grace.

"I don't know why you continue to harass and talk sh*t to me. I'm not the reason you and Daniel aren't together. I'm not even f*cking him."

My hands were in the surrender position. Grace charged towards me and punched me in my eye. I grabbed her shoulders and hair threw her to the ground. I landed on top of Grace and tried to punch her face into the floor. Grace somehow managed to get up and grabbed me by my hair. She held it as tight as she could with my face pointed toward the floor.

"Go get somebody before I kill this b*tch!"

"B*tch you better let my hair go."

Seconds later the manager, several men and women ran into the locker room, and Grace let my hair go.

"What's going on in here?"

Bill, the Operational Manager came in and questioned us.

"This is the woman I was talking about when I told Bryan one of your members was harassing and threatening me."

"Don't get mad because I'm driving your man's car."

"No b*tch. I'm not even dating him and haven't in months, so what are you talking about?"

Several other members gathered by the door leading to the locker room and listened in.

"Everybody, leave."

Bill pointed towards the locker room door.

"I want to press charges against her, so can you call the police?"

"Call the police for what. I was defending myself."

"What happened Kelley?"

Bill interjected.

"When I got off the treadmill, I spoke to Bryan and then I came in here. I told her I was not the reason Daniel didn't want her and she charged at me and punched me in the eye."

"That's not what happened. She came in here and walked in my face and I thought she was going to hit me so I defended myself."

*This b*tch is lying between her teeth and whatever she's up to; it's not going to work.* I thought.

"Can I call the police please?"

"Yes."

Two officers arrived. Officer Finley was short, slim, light-skinned, somewhat handsome, and maybe in his late thirties. Officer Davis was tall, dark-skinned, unattractive with a fat belly, a curly Afro, and maybe in his late forties. Both dressed in their CPD uniforms with their handcuffs, flashlight, club and a nine millimeter attached to their hips.

"What's the problem?"

Officer Finley started the conversation. Grace and I began talking.

"Wait a minute. Who called the police?"

"I did."

"What is your name, ma'am?"

"Kelley Porter."

"What is yours?"

"Grace Zolic."

"I need to see both of your I.D's. Bill can we get copies of their I.D's please?"

"Kelley what happened?"

"She has been harassing and threatening me for the last two years and today while I was on the treadmill, she approached me and threatened me."

"That's not what happened."

"Ma'am, when I'm ready for you to talk I will ask you. Take her to another room. Bill, can you take her into another room?"

"Sure."

"Go ahead Kelley."

"I told her to get the hell out of my face. When I finished on the treadmill, I told Bryan she was threatening me and he told me if she bothered me again to let him know."

"Who is Bryan?"

"He's one of our managers."

Bill interjected.

"Okay and how did this fight start?"
"When I came in the locker room, I talked to her at least twenty feet away and with my hands up in the air. Before I could say another word, she charged and punched me in my face. So I want to press charges against her."
"How do you know each other?"
"We were dating the same man and she thinks I'm the reason he doesn't want her. She has keyed my car, and threatened me while I was pregnant. She told me after I had my child, she was going to kick my ass."
"Who was he dating first?"
"Her. And for the last two years, she's blamed me for their problems."
"So she hit you first?"
"Yes, she did."
"Did anyone see this?"
"There were a few Hispanic women in here."
"I talked to the women that were in here, but they left. I got their phone numbers if you need them officer."
"Okay. Let's see what she has to say."

Officer Finley left the room and went to see what Grace had to say. Officer Davis came in the office and asked me the same questions and I repeated myself. Thereafter he and Officer Finley talked among each other and Office Davis decided he wasn't going to press charges against her.

"Why the hell not? I was defending myself and that b*tch just gets away with this."
"It was a fight so you're both lucky I don't take you to jail."
Officer Davis left the room.
"Kelley, here is a copy of her I.D. You can go down to the station on fifty-first and State Street and talk to them. Bill said there are witnesses and here are their phone numbers. Have a good day." Officer Finley felt differently about the ordeal.
"Thank you."

I don't know what this b*tch told them, but this sh*t is not over. This b*tch has been harassing me over two years and now she wants to fight me. It ain't over. I thought.

"Bill, am I going to lose my membership?"

"No, Kelley you're not. I talked to the women who were in the locker room and it was a one-sided story. But if you want her membership revoked, you can write a letter to the district manager."

"Okay. Can I have his information, please?"

"Sure. Here it is."

"Thank you."

I was furious. I called Daniel and told him what happened.

"Hello."

"Hey Daniel, I just got into a fight with Grace at the gym."

"What?! What happened?"

"When I was on the treadmill she came up to me talking sh*t and I told her to get the hell out of my face. So I went into the locker room to talk to her and she ran towards me and hit me in my face."

"Are you serious Kelley?"

"Yea, I wasn't trying to fight her. My hands were up in the air. I was just trying to talk to her. You really need to put her in line. I haven't had anything to do with you in over five months, so why the hell is she still bothering me? Crazy b*tch."

"She doesn't even go to the gym on Kedzie. She was on some bullshit from the beginning. Where are you now?"

"On my way home."

"Where is Shemar?"

"Mama has him at my place."

"Do you mind if I stop by?"

"That's fine."

"I'm about to call her ass right now."

"Bye."

I finally made it home.

"Hey Mama."

"Hey baby. What happened to your eye?"

"I got into a fight with Grace at the gym. All this time she has bothered me over a nigga. She should have been in his face not mine. Daniel told me she had a habit of approaching women. One time she got in some woman's face and the chick cut her over her eye with a razor blade. Crazy ass woman."

"Shemar is asleep and don't wake him."

"Okay."

My doorbell rang.

"Mama, could you let Daniel in?"

"Hey Kelley."

"Hey. Let me see your face. What the f*ck is wrong with her? I talked to her and there all kinds of holes in her story. I knew her ass lied."

"I have to go to the police station and file another report. She lied to the officers and they didn't believe me. I have the witnesses' phone numbers and the police gave me her I.D."

"Well, lock her ass up then. This sh*t is stupid as hell. Let me go. I will talk to you later."

The next day I went to the police station and filed the report. I gave the police Grace's job address, a copy of her photo I.D. and the witness phone number. Later that day, I received a phone call from the police and had to meet them back at the station. The police arrested Grace from her job and brought her to the police station. We met in one of the interrogation rooms and talked for about two hours about how the fight started. I repeated the entire incident to the police officers and gave them the witnesses' phone numbers. I was able to go ahead with the charges and have her arrested for battery. Her lies did not hold up this time. I received a court date, and afterwards, Grace had to complete over forty hours of community service. That satisfied me, but I didn't stop there. I wrote a letter to the Bally's district manager and he revoked her membership. I didn't care how long, just as long as she received punishment for what she did. I no longer had to see her face around my house or Bally's.

April 2002

Daniel invited me to his mother's birthday party and before I could enjoy myself, I had to defend myself. I really don't know what Ms. Harris had against me other than the fact that I was dating her son. I never disrespected her and in fact, I afraid to because I thought Daniel would leave me. She was very manipulative and did nothing but tell lies and cause problems. The sad part was, Daniel never believed me or he was in denial about who his mother really was.

"Why did you have that baby on Daniel when you knew he didn't want more kids?"
Ms. Harris's sister stepped out of line.
"Excuse me. You have no idea what you're talking about and since you think you know something, did you know I aborted my first child?" I grabbed my plate of food and walked away.
The nerve of this bi*ch. She has no idea what she's talking about. Ain't no one told her that sh*t but Ms. Harris fat ass and she knows damn well I aborted my first baby. I'm ready to get the hell out of here before I snap the f*ck off. I thought. I went downstairs to eat my food with the rest of the guests. I sat with Daniel's uncle and a few of his other kinsfolk.
"If you stop trying to control Daniel the relationship might work." Daniel's uncle decided he would get in our business.
"Who said I was trying to control him? Daniel does whatever he wants to do."
"I've been around a lot longer than you have and trying to control a man will run him away."

I was in total disbelief and never responded. I took my food upstairs, threw it in the garbage and walked outside. *This mama's boy ass nigga tells his mother everything. Lying f*cker. I'm not trying to control his ass. His fat, stinking ass mother is a liar. She knows damn well I aborted my first baby and she knows I told Daniel to use a condom. What the f*ck? I hate that b*tch and I should have never given his raggedy, bald mouth ass another chance. Both of them are lying, controlling and manipulative ass bastards.* I thought.
"What's wrong Kelley?"

"Nothing."
"Why are you standing out here?"
"I'm just smoking a cigarette."
"Kelley what's wrong?"
"You're not going to do anything."
"What happened?"
"Your damn aunt asked me *why I had a baby on you knowing you didn't want more kids.* I know your mother told her that sh*t. Your uncle said *I need to stop trying to control you.* Why are they saying anything to me? You talk too damn much. Is there anything you don't tell your damn mother?"
"What does she have to do with it?"
"Did you tell your aunt and uncle that sh*t? How do they know anything about our relationship? You told your mama about that control mess and she exaggerated the story about me having a baby with you when you didn't want any more. Do you take any responsibility for getting me pregnant three times? Did you tell them I just aborted another baby? You're the one who refused to use a condom after I told you I wanted a child. I didn't do this alone. This is some bullsh*t."
"My aunt and uncle said that to you?"
"That's what I said. Why the hell do I have to lie?" Why won't you ever say something to your mother?"
"I'm not going to disrespect my mother."
"I'm not asking you to. I'm asking you to tell her to mind her damn business and stop f*cking with me."
"Imma go talk to her. I'm sick of this too."
"You need to stop telling her all of your damn business."
Daniel walked into his mother's house and came back a few minutes later.
"I didn't see her in there. Maybe she's upstairs."
"I'm going home."
"I will leave with you."

I was completely blown away when Daniel chose to leave with me and not stay with his mother. That didn't last long. Daniel claimed he wanted to do things differently to make our relationship better. He put Grace out of his house and said he wanted me. I wasn't sure if I believed him. Daniel was a lying and deceptive man who was only out for himself. He was very selfish and anytime he did something for you he made certain to remind you of it. No one came before his mother and that included his children. We spent the rest of the spring and summer as a couple, but it wasn't without the same lies, betrayal and deceit. Daniel was a complete womanizer, but I was in love with him. We did a lot of partying, dining, movies, shooting pool and shopping together. I thought things were going great, but what was to come; felt like karma.

December 2002
"Kelley, I don't see a baby in your uterus."
I asked my friend Kim, who was also a radiologist to do an Ultrasound on me.
"Why? I haven't had a period in two months. I know I'm pregnant."
"I understand that. Wait a minute. The baby is growing in your Fallopian tube."
"What does that mean?"
"It's called an ectopic pregnancy and it's very dangerous. You need to see your doctor right away."
"Will my baby be okay?"
"Kelley, go see your doctor immediately. If this baby continues to grow, your Fallopian tube can rupture and you can die. Just go straight to E.R."
"Okay."
I left work and drove directly to Dr. Watson's office.
"Hi Dr. Watson, I'm not scheduled for today, but I have an ectopic pregnancy."
"Who told you that?"
"The Radiologist at my job said she didn't see a baby in my uterus and it was growing in my tube."

"I see. I'm going to write an order for you to go over to Trinity now and have another Ultrasound. When you're done, come back here."
"Okay."
Trinity hospital confirmed the diagnosis and Dr. Watson told me if I had any shoulder pain to go to the emergency room immediately. I didn't even bother telling Daniel. I knew he wouldn't care. He never wanted any of the kids I was pregnant with. The next day, I stared in the mirror and cried. I wanted this child and had already lost it. As I wiped my tears, I felt a sharp pain in my shoulder. I immediately drove to Trinity hospital and the ER doctor admitted me. I awoke with an I.V in my arm and fluids connected. I felt extremely groggy and realized one of the IV fluid bags was morphine. I looked around and no one was there. There was a TV hanging from the ceiling displaying the news. The colorful curtain prevented me from seeing who was on the other side of my bed. I tried to sit up and screamed. The pain in my lower abdominal area was excruciating. I cried and pressed the red button.

"Are you okay over there?"
The other patient worried.
"I'm okay."
"Ms. Porter did you need something?"
My nurse came in the room.
"I want to see Dr. Watson. This pain is killing me."
"Dr. Watson will be back at around seven pm and he will be in to see you. When you can't tolerate the pain, press this button and you will relax."
"Okay."
"If you need anything else Ms. Porter, ring the bell."
"Okay."
I pressed that button connected to my I.V and minutes later I was asleep again.
"Ms. Porter, Ms. Porter, Kelley."
"Yes. Hi Dr. Watson."

"Hi Ms. Porter. I need to share something with you. I did surgery on you and we removed the tube that carried the baby and there was also a blood clot. But while I was examining your uterus and Fallopian tubes, I noticed there was a blood clot in your other tube. Kelley, I have known you since you were a teenager as well as your whole family. I didn't want to take a chance and leave the blood clot and later it detaches, travel and possibly kill you. So I talked to a few of the other surgeons and doctors, and decided to remove both tubes. I'm really sorry. It was a very hard choice for me. I can't imagine if something happened later and we lost you. I thought long and hard about it. I'm really sorry Kelley."
"So this means I can't have any more children."
"You can have kids. There is nothing wrong with your eggs. I didn't remove them, but you would need to have a procedure called…
"In vitro fertilization?"
I interrupted Dr. Watson.
"Yes."
I dropped my head and cried.
"I'm only 31 and wanted another baby. I should have just kept the ones I aborted."
"Kelley you did what you thought was best. Don't have regrets. Now don't forget you can still have another baby just not through the normal conception."
I cried because I knew it was over. Daniel wasn't even interested in Shemar so I knew I would never have another child. I cried and cried.
"Kelley I will let you get some rest and come back to see you in the morning."
"Good Morning Kelley. How are you feeling?"
Dr. Watson came back as he said he would.
"I'm better."
"If you want to see to a therapist, I can set you up with someone."
"No. I'm fine."
"Okay. We drew some blood from you and your test levels were normal. In a couple of days you should have a bowel movement. At that time we will discharge you."

"That's fine."
"Let me check your wound and I will let you get some rest."
"Okay."

Dr. Watson examined me and everything looked okay. He discharged me two days later and I went home. Shemar was with Mama and I was off work, and school for six weeks. During that time I did a lot of thinking. I concluded if I had allowed the doctor to explore my womb after I had that ruptured cyst, she would have noticed the blood clots and maybe gave me medicine to dissolve them. I realized if it was meant for my baby to live, it would have. I had to pick myself up and keep going for Shemar, school and work, but I wasn't prepared for what was to come.

Inability to Walk – 6

February 2004
I went to see my doctor at the University of Chicago Hospital and that visit was one of many I could have done without. The nurse called me to the back.
"I'm having this pain in my spine that travels down my legs and around to the front of my thighs."
"Were you lifting anything?"
"Yes, at work. My boss asked me to move these fifty-five pound containers."
"Okay."
"We're going to do an X-ray and then an MRI."
"Okay."
The pain I felt was something unusual. My right thigh felt very weak and I could not sit or stand for long periods of time. I was unable to bend over and sometimes I lost feeling in my foot. Over the next year and four months my life plummeted to rock bottom again. My doctor diagnosed me with a bulging disc in my spine as well as foramina stenosis. There was always pressure on the nerves in my lumbar spine that lead to numbness in my foot along with leg and back pain that disabled me.

After I left Little Company of Mary Hospital, Antech Diagnostics, an animal laboratory hired me. My boss asked me to reposition these fifty-five pound Biohazard waste containers. After months of moving these containers, I began to have back pain. I wasn't certain if it was my kidneys or typical back pain. But after my third doctor's appointment, I learned it was more than I was able to bear. I sat on the hospital bed and waited for Dr. Fish to come in. There were two interns present, a nurse and a Radiologist. The interns prepped the Mayo stand with Betadine, Lidocaine, syringes, gauze and bandages.
"Kelley I understand you're allergic to IVP dye correct."
Janice was Dr. Fish's nurse.
"Yes."
"What actually happens after you receive this dye?"

"I get hives in my face."

"Okay. I'm going to start an I.V with Benadryl, and this is to prevent any allergic reaction from the dye. The dye enhances the doctor's abilities to see the injection area. You will feel a little drowsy, but we need you to stay awake so we know we're in the right place."

"Okay."

"Hi Kelley."

Dr. Fish walked in.

"Hi Dr. Fish, I don't want the interns to inject me. I want you to do it."

"That's fine Kelley. Go ahead and lie down on your stomach, and we will place this pillow under your legs."

"Okay."

The Radiologist positioned the machine over my back and I could feel something cold and wet. I assumed it was the Betadine.

"Kelley are you still awake?"

"Yes, I am."

"Kelley you're going to feel some pain now as we inject the Lidocaine to numb this area."

I cringed and clenched my teeth tightly.

"Are you okay?"

"Yea."

Janice stood at the head of my bed and rubbed my hand. I wanted the pain to go away and prayed this injection would work.

"Kelley I'm now going to inject the cortisol, and I need you to tell me which leg you feel a sensation following the path of your pain."

"Okay."

"Do you feel anything?"

"No. Wait. I felt that on the left side."

"Good, that means we are in the right area."

"I felt that on the right side."

"Great. We're going to do one more injection and we're all done."

"Okay. We're done Kelley. My nurse will get you all cleaned up and take you to the recovery room. I will check on you in about twenty minutes to see how you feel."
"Okay. Thanks Dr. Fish."
I awoke in severe pain screaming. The nurses ran into the room and I crying. There was no relief. My doctor rescheduled an appointment in one month and discharge me. I tried to take care of Shemar, attend work and school, but the pain was getting worse as the days went by.

"Can you please send an ambulance to 12555 S. Aberdeen Street?" Mama called the ambulance. I lied on my back having severe spasms as the tears rolled down my face. I could not move. I felt paralyzed. I cried and cried. This was the worst pain I ever experienced.

"Somebody help my mama. You want some candy?"
I tried to smile, but the pain wasn't giving in. The paramedics arrived and when they tried to pick me up, I screamed. They stood back with sad looks on their faces.
"I'm so sorry sweetie. Let us know when we can move you."
"She's having really bad back spasms. She's can't move. We need to get the stretcher. Sweetie, we're going to lay the stretcher on the floor next to you and when you're ready, just roll over or try to scoot over on it. Take your time."

I slowly tried to scoot on the stretcher and it felt like an hour passed. Finally, I was on the stretcher and when the paramedic lifted it, I screamed to the top of my lungs. My neighbor opened her door to see what was wrong. Mama spoke with her as she held Shemar. Every step down those two flights of stairs was hell. It felt like someone was stabbing and twisting a knife in my spine. The pain was sharp and shooting down the back of my legs. My right thigh was weak and my foot felt very cold. The Paramedics took me to St. Francis Hospital and I was treated me with morphine. I slept for hours and when I awoke, the pain wasn't as bad. Nicki picked me up from the hospital. We made it to my place and she helped me up the stairs. I slowly walked to my bedroom and crawled in the bed with Mama and Shemar. I awoke the next day and without any pain.

April 2004
"Hey Nicki, I'm in the emergency room again."
"For your back again?"
"Yep, Daniel said if you meet him at my house, he will take you to my job to pick my car up."
"Okay. That's cool. I'm on my way."
"Okay. I'm going to call him. Thanks."
"Hey Daniel, Nicki said she's on her way to my place."
"Okay. I'm on my way over there and I will stop at the hospital on the way back."
"Okay. Bye."

Daniel and Nicki stopped by the hospital to visit and Nicki waited for me. Mama was at home with Shemar. The pain, constant emergency room visits, and trips to the pain clinic really depressed me. There was nothing the doctor's in the emergency room could do for me other than give me morphine for the pain. They discharged me a few hours later. Mama, my niece Janae, Nicki and Daniel were regulars around my house. Janae practically lived with me for a while to help me with Shemar. Daniel decided father Shemar when he wanted to. I was in no place to argue or fight with him. My energy was very low and I couldn't deal with the fights.

July 2004
Daniel decided he wanted to get married so we purchased rings, but we didn't set a date. We took family photos and began to behave as a couple. I really didn't know what he wanted with me knowing my condition. I was always moody and at any given time I would cry. Some days I could walk and some days I could not. This was a very trying time for me and I wasn't sure of myself.

Janae took me to the hospital and I didn't have an appointment. She helped me downstairs because I was no longer able to walk. I slithered around my place like a snake. If I got in the tub, I was unable to get out without help. If I used the toilet, I needed help getting up. I couldn't stand for longer than an hour. I couldn't sit for longer than thirty minutes. I was no longer able to do simple daily activities. Some days, Daniel or Janae dropped me off and picked me up from school. My ability to walk was unstable. I couldn't sit or stand for too long. I took twelve pills a day for pain. I went from independent to dependent. Each day the pain got worse and eventually I was on bed rest.

****

"I want to see Dr. Fish right f*cking now! I'm sick of this sh*t. I can't walk."
The secretary ran to the back and Dr. Fish's nurse came out.
"Hi Kelley, Dr. Fish will be out in a minute. You don't have an appointment so we can't inject you today."
"She's going to do something. I can't walk."
"I will see what we can do."
"Kelley. Come on back."
"Dr. Fish, I can't walk. I can't feel my foot hit the ground. I can't sit down. I can't stand up. I can't drive. I can't take a bath. This pain in my leg breaks me down. I can't take this. Please help me. Please give me something. I can't take this pain anymore."
"I will squeeze you in now and try a Selective Nerve Block."
"Okay."
"It's okay Aunt. Don't cry."
"Janae, I can't take this. This pain is horrible. I just want it to go away."
Dr. Fish performed the nerve block and it worked. Finally, discharged home with no pain.
"How are you feeling Kelley?"
Daniel stopped by to see me.
"I feel good. That nerve blocked worked. I haven't had any pain in a couple of weeks."

After a few weeks passed, I went out with Daniel and the pain came back. From that day forward and each time I tried to go outside, someone had to carry me from my destination, or wheel me out in a wheel chair. I went through bottles of Valium, Vicadin, Zanaflex, Darvoxet, Celebrex, and Neurontin. Many times I slept days away. My weight dropped down to one hundred and twenty-five pounds. I was angry, depressed and confused. The entire summer was pain medicine, wheelchairs and depending upon others. I didn't want to live with that pain. It was unbearable. I didn't want to live and not walk on my own. I didn't want to live, and burden everybody else.

I walked with a limp some days, and some I couldn't walk at all. My doctor realized working was a problem so he took me off work for weeks at a time. I could barely pay my bills. I felt dead on the inside.

January 2005
"Hi Ms. Porter."
"Hi Doctor Lieber."
"I'm going to take you off work and put you on bed rest. I'm really sorry this has happened to you. Kelley you will probably never run again, and as you get older you will more than likely lose your ability to walk."

I cried. I felt like my life was over. That was the worse news I ever heard. I injured my entire spine when I pushed and pulled those containers. I never knew when the pain would hit me. My biggest fear was to drive, and lose feeling in my foot, or have spasms in my back. I received almost thirty injections in my spine and had taken practically every pain medicine. Nothing really worked. I could no longer pay any bills, but Daniel stepped in and helped out tremendously. I had a separate insurance on my car that covered disability and it lasted for one year.
Whatever was left from my student loans, I used it to pay the bills Daniel didn't pay. He worked twelve-hour days and on a

monthly basis, he gave me about seven hundred to a thousand dollars. Daniel felt like since he was paying my bills, he could sex with him when he wanted. I didn't understand his selfishness and lack of compassion. He continued to pay my bills for about six months and I gave up.

May 2005
I somehow managed to graduate from Chicago State University. I wasn't enthused at all. I received a one year scholarship for outstanding achievement as well as a perseverance award. Many days I went to school and laid on the desk suffering in pain. I refused to give up. I was proud of myself for finishing, but what was next for me. I realized my dream of being a nurse was daddy's dream for me. As a child, I dreamt of being a surgeon. Daddy always talked to me about being a nurse so I thought I would. I became so focused on what daddy wanted for me, I forgot about being a surgeon. I was confused about what I wanted to do. I was very indecisive. I selected a career I didn't know much about or care about. I've always been a hands on type of person and Health Information Management was not for me. My biggest concern was what was next for me after graduation. I could barely stand on my own two feet, let alone seek employment in a field I wasn't interested in. I became increasingly afraid to go outside or do anything that required driving. I felt like my life was over.

July 2005
"Daniel, I'm going to move in with Yolanda so you don't have to worry about paying my bills anymore."
"That's fine because it's getting real hard on me."
"I told you months ago to stop and I could've moved back home, but I appreciate all of your help."

I decided to sell our wedding rings because I knew I wasn't going to marry Daniel. He never changed. I was no longer able to pay my bills and after six years of living in Calumet Park, I moved to Harvey, Illinois with Yolanda. I tried to hide my pain from Shemar, but many days I snapped at him out of anger and pain. Shemar was the only person who kept me happy, but after losing everything, I was no longer the mother I remembered. I will never forget the day I yelled at him when he was three years old, and he said, *I want my mama back.* I cried, held him and apologized. Being crippled, tarnished my heart and faith. I slept on Yolanda's couch for three months. I bought food with my link card and tried to supply whatever I could. Although I wasn't able to work, I still looked for a job hoping I would be fine.

The transmission died in my car and that added to my depression. Daniel had it towed to Toyota on sixty-ninth and Western where it sat for six months. I knew the manager so they held my car for me without any extra storage fees. Daniel paid the nine hundred and eighty dollars to have my car fixed. Many days Shemar and I spent nights with him at his mother's house. He lost his house due to child support and moved in with his mother. I hated the sight of that woman and even more after she stepped across the line with my son.

September 2005
"Daniel how did Shemar get this bruise in his face?"
"Mama said it was a reflex."
"A reflex? Why did she hit him? Did she apologize?"
"I don't know. She said Shemar told her he was going to kill me."
"He's three years old. He doesn't even understand the word kill, so why would he use it?"
"I don't know. That's what Mama said."
I packed our things and shared my feelings with Daniel. I was angry, so I knew the best thing for me to do was to leave.
 "You got something to say to my mother, you got something to say to my mother?"
Instead of Daniel talking to his mother, he decided to lead his mother directly to me and it wasn't pretty. I had flashbacks of how that woman treated me and I snapped.

"You got something to say to me?"

Ms. Harris stood in the doorway of Daniel's bedroom.
"As a matter of fact, I do. I told your ass I didn't want you hitting my son in the face. If you had to spank him, spank his ass not his face."
"He's a damn heathen, and he doesn't listen."
"B*tch I tell you and every motherf*cker in here. I will kill all you motherf*ckers if you ever touch my son again. What the f*ck do you want? You ain't got sh*t to do with this so take your ass back upstairs!"

Ms. Harris's boyfriend came downstairs and stood in the doorway.
Daniel you are a b*tch ass nigga. What type of man allows his mother to slap his child? You ain't sh*t. Punk ass bastard."

"He's more man than you will ever be a woman."
"You fat b*tch. You don't even know him as a man. You know him as a f*cking mama's boy."
Shemar screamed and cried. I tried to comfort him, but I was furious.
"I bet my son doesn't come to your mother's house and disrespect her."
"You don't know what your trifling ass son does. Punk ass motherf*cker. You lucky I don't f*ck all y'all asses up."
"You can get out my house."
"I'm not going anywhere b*tch. You can feel free to call the police so I can have your fat ass arrested. I will leave when my f*cking ride gets here."
Daniel sat there with this stupid look on his face. I wanted to kill him and his mother. I was under enough stress to cause everybody in that house bodily harm.
"I'm trying to keep him from going to prison."
Ms. Harris was on the phone talking to her sister.
"You fat f*cker, he's only three years old! Daniel you are truly a b*tch ass nigga."
"You better hurry up and get the hell out."
"What the hell are you going to do? You ain't gonna do sh*t so shut the f*ck up. When my ride comes I will leave."

Nicki blew the horn and I left. She dropped me off at Yolanda's house. I realized if Daniel couldn't defend me and protect his son, there was nothing he could do for me. I ended that relationship and never looked at him the same. It was one thing for him to never defend me, but to allow his mother to hit his son, leave a bruise and he does nothing. That was not the type of man I wanted to marry. I was not interested in giving Daniel another chance after that day. I wasn't able to leave Daniel for me, but my son meant everything to me and through him, I was able to cut that relationship off.

****

Back at Yolanda's house things were going pretty well until she told me I had to move.
"Kelley my boyfriend is moving in around Christmas. So you will have to move by then."
"Okay, that's fine. I will just go ahead and get my stuff together now."
"You don't have to go now. You have until December."
"Naw, it's cool. I can just go live with Chrissy. I appreciate you helping me."
I called Chrissy and asked her if I could live with her for a few months and she didn't mind. I packed my belongings and moved out.

October 2005
Shemar and I moved in with Chrissy. We slept in her back room on a blow up bed. I bought food and kept her house clean. Daniel dropped Shemar off at daycare every day and maintained my phone bill. He let me borrow his van so I could get around from time to time. Daniel helped me a lot and I appreciated his help and time. He wasn't obligated to do anything for me. He was only obligated to take care of Shemar.

I was really depressed, but tried to smile every day. I never wanted to live with Chrissy. We still didn't get along, but I humbled myself and stayed out of her way. She was at work most of the day and evening so that wasn't hard. I didn't ask for anything and anytime I went outside, I asked my nephew Ty to keep Shemar. Chrissy tried to support and comfort me, and I appreciated the concern. That concern didn't last too long. After about two months of living with Chrissy it all came to a loud and stormy end.

"I don't think the babies should call another man daddy. Their father will be back."
"That doesn't matter. He ain't here now."
I was talking to Janae, and Chrissy decided to share her opinion.
"Y'all just ignorant."
"Ignorant. If we're ignorant you can get the f*ck out. Get the f*ck out my house."
"I will leave. I don't give a sh*t."
It was about five inches of snow outside and very cold. I grabbed my coat and was on my way out the door at three o'clock in the morning.
"Take your f*cking son with you."
"I'm not waking my baby up to take him out in that sh*t."
"I will call the police."
"You're kidding me. Shemar has nothing to do with this."
I cried.
"I don't give a f*ck. He has to leave too."
"Hahahahaha. Look at your ass now."
Chrissy laughed and so did everyone else.

Earlier that night, Janae invited some friends over and we were drinking and playing cards. Janae, Chrissy and I disagreed during a conversation, and at three o'clock in the morning, Chrissy threw me out of her house in the middle of winter with Shemar. I cried as I packed my son up. The police arrived and they didn't understand why Shemar had to leave. It was very cold outside and Daniel's van wasn't all that reliable. *She is one dirty b*tch and she will get hers.* I thought. I cried all the way from the south side to Mama's place in Riverdale.

"Hey baby. What are you doing out at this time of night?" What happened?

"Me, Janae and Chrissy had an argument and Chrissy threw me and Shemar out."

"Her ass did me like that at one o'clock in the morning all because she claims I left her door open and didn't do the dishes."

Nicki was angry.

"Why didn't she let Shemar stay?"

"I don't know. She told me to wake him up and take him with me."

"What the hell is wrong with her?"

I took Shemar in mama's room and laid him down. Damenia, Nicki and I sat up for a while and talked. I told Mama I needed a place to stay and she didn't have a problem with me living with her. The next day, I drove back to Chrissy's place to get the rest of our clothing. I called Chrissy and left many vulgar messages on her voice mail.

You are one ignorant b*tch and you wonder why don't nobody wanna be bothered with your ass and that includes your damn daughter. You treat people like sh*t and think people wanna be bothered with your ass. You're going to find yourself alone and f*cking miserable. F*cking b*tch. I hung the phone up and didn't speak to Chrissy for months.

"Hello."

"Hey Daniel."

"Hey Kelley, what's up?"

"I'm at Mama's house now."

"Why are you at your mother's house?"

"Chrissy put me and Shemar out."

"When?"

"Last night at about three in the morning."

"Kelley I don't mean no harm, but she is f*cked up. Who the f*ck would do that to someone in the middle of the winter with a baby? She ain't gonna ever have any luck; then to treat my baby like that, f*ck her. She ain't ever liked you no way. You should have moved with granny in the first place, but there really ain't no room. Where are you going to sleep?"

"In the room with Mama."

"That's messed up she would do that to you. I will be by later to see baby Mar."

"That's fine. I have to go by her house and get the rest of my stuff."

"Okay, call me when you're done."

Daniel was far from my man. I couldn't stand the sight of him. But I needed help. He continued to give me money and help me in any way he could. He always visited and checked on me. I really didn't want anything from him. I wanted him to leave me alone. Eventually I got my wish.

Cutting Ties – 7

December 2005

I stayed with Mama for about eight months and those were the best, yet worst eight months of my life. Damenia was on drugs and Nicki was depressed. No one knew I was at the end of my rope. I tried to distract myself by focusing on Mama and everything else that was going on. Too many days we argued and cussed each other out. Some days we had fun, and others, I wanted them to leave me alone. I had to take Shemar out of daycare for a little while. My car was still in the shop and I still suffered from the spinal injury. The visits to the pain clinic were never ending.

Most of the time, I sat in Mama's room and played with Shemar. He was my only light. His smile kept me going many days. The stress behind Damenia's addiction and aggressive behavior added to my pain. She always threatened to hit Mama and I called the police on her. Nicki was very fickle, and some days would instigate an argument between Damenia and me. She was only concerned about her crack head boyfriend. Nicki showed me a different side and made me not trust her. I hated the sight of them. I hated how they treated and disrespected Mama, especially Damenia.

"I will be so glad when her ass stop using drugs. She comes in at all times of the night banging on the door. Her crack head ass gets on my nerves."
Nicki never replied, but later that day she told Damenia what I said.
"B*tch, I know you ain't in here talking sh*t about me. I ought to knock the sh*t out of you."
"You ain't going to do a damn thing to me."

I sat in the kitchen at Shemar's red, blue and green octagon table. I
looked at Nicki in disbelief. She and I were close or so I thought. We both talked about Damenia, and her drug use on

many occasions, but I never ran back and told Damenia anything.

"If you put your f*cking hands on me, I will have your ass arrested."

"That's what the f*ck you gonna have to do. B*tch."

"You really need to get the f*ck away from me."

"What the hell is going on?!"

Mama walked in the kitchen.

"Nicki ran back and told Damenia I was talking about her and now she's in here threatening me."

"Ain't no fighting going on in here. Damenia, get your ass on somewhere."

"I ain't going no f*cking where."

"Mama, I will call the police on her if she hits me."

I got up and went into Mama's room, closed the door and cried. I hated Nicki for what she did and wished Damenia would leave and never come back. I felt like they didn't want me there or was jealous. They knew I wasn't going to allow them to mistreat Mama any longer. Nicki and Damenia didn't realize I was just as depressed and miserable as they were. All I wanted was for them to show Mama the respect she deserved. They had nothing but resentment in them for Mama. Nicki was no different from Damenia. Her level of respect was at an all-time low for Mama. She always pretended she was nice, kind and respectful. I learned later she was truly a phony person. Between her telling Damenia what I said, and the days to come, I saw Nicki in a different light.

"Why do you have his ass in Mama's house?"

"Get the f*ck away from my door."

I talked to Nicki while her door was closed.

"Tell that nigga to find somewhere to go."

"You got your ass here so now what. You ain't got sh*t."

"And I'm here because I'm off work. What's your damn reason? You got his ass lying up in Mama's house and then don't wanna take her to the damn hospital. Sorry ass."

"Yep, and your ass have Daniel over here too."

"Visiting, but not living."

I went out that night and had a few cocktails and learned Nicki's boyfriend, John was living there as well. Mama never wanted him there and in fact, she didn't want any of them there. But since she didn't have much money, she allowed John to live there and he paid her one hundred dollars a month. John was an abusive addict and I did not want him living in my mother's house.

January 2006
Daniel made the last payment on my Camry and we picked it up from Toyota. I was so grateful. Everybody knew we were not dating and he was just helping. I actually began to hate the sight of him. I dealt with him because of Shemar and I needed help. Every now and then he would ask for sex and more than often, I told him *no*. I lost my attraction to him. Everything he did to me made me resent him and the thought of sleeping with him grossed me out. He didn't even look like the same handsome man I met seven years ago. His appearance was the same, but I never saw him in the same light after he allowed his mother to slap Shemar. I accepted all the things Daniel did to me, but I refused to allow him to treat my son like anything other than an innocent child.

This particular day I had no pain, so I decided to go to Geno's. I drank more than usual as always. I wanted to forget about the past year. I wanted my ability to walk freely. I wanted the pain to go away. I wanted to stop taking all the medicine and I wanted freedom from the injections. I wanted my independence back. I wanted my life back. I didn't want to suffer any no longer and I wanted to die. I made it home drunk and staggering. I could barely walk up the three flights of stairs. I went in Mama's room, close the door and began to cry. *I can't take this anymore. I'm tired of suffering and being in pain. What did I do to deserve this? When is this going to end? What did I do wrong?* I thought.

Kelley Porter

*Hi. I can't deal with any of this anymore. I'm ending this now.
Kelley*

I wrote a suicide note and left it in the kitchen on Shemar's octagon table. I took about ten to fifteen Darvocet pills, went in Mama's room, and sat on the floor. Minutes later, Damenia knocked on the door and I let her in. Coming home on a Saturday night was something Damenia never did and Nicki rarely opened her bedroom door when she was asleep.

"Nicki, Nicki, come here! Look at this!"
Nicki came out of her bedroom and Damenia showed her my letter.
"Kelley what is this?"
"She's trying to kill has damn self!"
Mama awoke from all the commotion.
"Kelley did something! I think she's trying to kill herself! She left this damn note right here!"
Nicki gave my note to Mama.
"Kelley what have you done? Oh my God. Kelley. Kelley what did you do?"
"I took a bunch of Darvocet."
I dropped my head.
"Got damn it, call the ambulance!"
A few minutes later the police arrived and so did the paramedics. Shemar awoke and I instantly cried.
"Little man, you have to step outside of the room."
The police officer wanted to talk to me alone.
"No mommy."
"It's okay, peanut. It's okay. Just go stand right there and Mommy will be right out."
"Did you write this letter?"
"Yea."
"What did you do? Did you take some pills?"
"I took some Darvocet."

The paramedics immediately led me out the house and into the ambulance. Shemar screamed and it felt like my heart dropped out of my chest. They took me to Ingalls hospital and the doctors gave me some charcoal to swallow to prevent my liver from absorbing the Darvocet. One of the nurses told me had I not got there when I did, my liver would have failed leading to death. Damenia, Nicki and Mama stopped in and hugged me. I stayed a night in the hospital and was then transferred to the Ingalls Behavioral Health Center. This center was nothing like Tinley Park. I shared a room with another inpatient and it was very similar to a hospital room. There were no bars and cots. The dining area was pretty and warm, not cold and emotionless. I was able to talk and mingle with the other inpatients, but we were always monitored by someone. If we wanted to go out and take a smoke, one of the employees chaperoned with us. Each day was tears and pain.

"Kelley the doctor wants to see you."
"Okay."
"Hi Ms. Porter."
"Hi."
"Would you like to share with me why you tried to commit suicide?"
"It's just too much stress in my mother's house and my family was being very mean to me."
I dropped my head and cried.
"I see. Is that all you want to share?"
"Yes."
"Ms. Porter I will be back to see you tomorrow."
I left his office and went back into my room. I cried for the rest of the day. Each day in that hospital was filled with tears and not much talking. I really didn't want to eat with or talk to anyone. The only time I really came out of that room was to smoke a cigarette. I was really depressed. After a year of going to therapy to learn how to deal with the physical pain, I still wasn't able to gain control of the depressed state I was in.

By the end of day two, I shared more information with the behavioral specialist. I left my room and ate one meal on this day and went back into my room. Later that evening, the behavioral specialist came in my room to talk to me.

"Hi Ms. Porter."
"Hi."
"If you want to go home, you have to stop crying and be strong. Be strong and tell the doctor what really happened. If you don't, you will stay in here for a while. You have a son at home that needs you so get yourself together and tell the doctor the truth."
"Okay."
"You will see him in the morning."
"Okay."
I cried myself to sleep. The next morning after breakfast, it was time for me to see the doctor.
"Kelley the doctor is ready to see you now."
I walked into his office with a little more confidence. I knew I had to get out of this place. I stayed strong.
"Hi Ms. Porter."
"Hi doctor."
I smiled. I remained as calmly as I could. The behavioral specialist was right about Shemar needing me. I held my tears back and told the doctor everything he wanted to know.
"Why did you attempt suicide?"
"A year and half ago I was injured and eventually lost my ability to walk. I've had over 40 injections in my spine, physical therapy, a Tens Interferential Unit, heat therapy, pain medicines and nothing worked. The pain was so bad, I couldn't work so my doctor put me on bed rest. Sometimes I didn't feel my foot hit the ground and would fall. Eventually, I had to give up my apartment and move back home with my mother. It's too much stress there and I just couldn't take any more pain. I have a son that needs me and I regret my decision. I promise it will never happen again. I just wanted the pain to stop. It's so crippling."
"Okay. So how is the pain now?"
"It comes and goes. But my doctor prescribed me some Darvocet and it actually works better than any of the other medicine."
"Isn't that the same medicine you took when you attempted suicide?"
"Yes."

"What if the pain becomes unbearable again?"

"Doctor I'm not going to try to kill myself anymore. I want to live. After a year and a half of severe back and leg pain, anybody would want to give up. It was just hard. I've never experienced pain that bad before. But even if the pain was like that again, I don't want to die. My baby needs me and I love him. I wanted him. My mother is very helpful so if I need to cry, I will cry on my mother, but I will not attempt suicide again."

"Okay. I will come back and see you tomorrow and if everything is the same, you can go home."

"Okay, thank you.

I called Daniel and shared the news. Although we were not dating, Daniel was always there for me. He was a horrible boyfriend, but he was a good person.

The phone rang.

"Hello."

"Hey Daniel, the doctor said I can come home tomorrow so will you please come get me."

"Sure."

"I miss Shemar. How is he doing?"

"He's okay. He's been crying because he wants you."

"Can you bring him up here to see me?"

"Will they let me?"

"Yea, but he can't come in. I can just kiss and hug him through the door."

"Okay, I'm on my way."

"Thank you."

I held my tears back. I missed my baby so much. It had only been three days and it felt like I was away from Shemar forever.

"Hey Peanut."

Daniel finally made it and I squatted to hug Shemar.

"Hey Mommy."

"You can't go out that door."

The security guard watched me.

"I'm not. I'm hugging my son."

"You're going to have to close the door."

"Can you give me a minute, please?"

I cried.
I hugged and kissed Shemar and he cried. I didn't want to let him go. I went back to my room and cried. *There is no way in hell I'm staying in here another day beyond tomorrow. I need my baby and he needs me. I'm getting the hell out of here. What the hell was I thinking? I can't leave Shemar. Who will take care of him? I promise I will never attempt suicide again. I don't care how bad the pain gets. I need to live for my baby.* I thought. I went to sleep early that night. When I awoke, it was time to see the doctor again. By noon, the psychologist discharged me back home with my baby.

****

"Hey Mama."
"Hey baby girl. How are you feeling?"
"I'm okay."
I really wasn't, but I didn't want mama to worry. Before night fell, Nicki, Damenia and I had another argument. I called the police and asked them to take me to a shelter. I could not live under the same roof as them. Mama didn't want me to leave, but I knew I needed to get away from them.

I spent a night at a shelter in Palos Hills and after telling the counselors my story, they felt I shouldn't be there. I knew I didn't belong there, but I wanted to be away from the stress at Mama's house. I went back to Mama's place and decided to avoid Nicki and Damenia all together. Many times they asked me to come out of the room, but I refused. I decided it was time for me to disconnect from them. I had to cut my ties and move forward. Some days I tried to enjoy them, but it was always drama. Whenever days passed and Damenia couldn't get high, she became very angry and violent. She always targeted Mama or me, but I brought that to a halt. She never got in Nicki's face. I guess somewhere inside of her, she knew Nicki would kick her ass.

"F*ck you, get the f*ck out my face!"
Damenia, and Mama argued.

"You get the f*ck out my house!"
"I ain't going anywhere. Put me the f*ck out."
"Damenia, you really need to watch your damn mouth."
"What the f*ck are you going to do?!"
"Keep talking sh*t and you will find out."
"Kelley, I ain't worried about your ass. Shit. F*ck you too."
"Your ass is mad because you can't get high and now you're angry."
Nicki stayed in her room as she always did. When I saw Damenia get in Mama's face, that was more than enough for me.
"Nine one one where's your emergency?"
"14555 South Tracy in Riverdale."
"What's the problem ma'am?"
"This female is at my mother's house threatening her and she's high off drugs."
"Okay. We're on our way."
Minutes later the police arrived and Damenia behaved as she did nothing wrong. Mama was afraid to have her put out. So I took over. I spoke to the officers and Mama agreed with me. Damenia
left and had to stay gone for three days.

"Kelley you ain't did sh*t."
"I did enough. You're leaving aren't you? Ignorant ass."
"Calm down and just get your stuff."

The police officer interjected. Mama and I sat on the couch in silence and waited patiently for Damenia to leave. She finally left and the next three days were peaceful, and quiet. We didn't have to worry about her ringing the doorbell at three o'clock in the morning, or beating on the door like a manic. Mama was able to get some rest. Those three days passed, but things were a little different with Damenia's behavior. She knew from that day, I would call the police on her so she left on her own. I had to take control and protect Mama. Nicki wasn't doing anything. But I knew if Damenia hit Mama, Nicki would beat her ass. Nicki was just so depressed, and wrapped up into her boyfriend so her bedroom became her safe haven.

February 2006
The next few months were abusive arguments, depressed energy and more drama. I hated the sight of Nicki and Damenia. I loved them both, but at this time, I didn't trust either one of them. Some days were good, but more days were hell. The best part of living in that house was sleeping in the same bed with Mama, and having late night chats with her.

"Get the f*ck out of my room before I knock the sh*t out of you!"
Nicki yelled to the top of her lungs.
"What the hell? We can't talk?"
"I ain't got sh*t to say to you. Now get the f*ck out of my room."
I stood there staring at Nicki as my heart pounded through my chest.
"Get out of my room!"
"Kelley, come out of her room."
Mama came in Nicki's room to find out what was going on.
"All this damn yelling and screaming, but we can't talk, and settle this."
"F*ck you, I don't want to talk to you."
I walked out of Nicki's room and was shocked she threatened to hit me. She was very angry and mad because I didn't want her boyfriend living in Mama's apartment. He had no right to be there. He was a crack head just like Damenia. I didn't care if he paid Mama one hundred dollars. I did not want him there and he had to leave and he did.

I wasn't in as much pain these days as before. I hadn't received an injection in four months and that was great progress. I decided to diligently look for employment and focus on getting better. I went on job interviews week after week, and some called back and others didn't. I never gave up. I took advantage of all the days I didn't feel the pain. I avoided Damenia and Nicki as much as possible. I wanted them gone. I couldn't stand the arguments, disrespect, threats, fear, noise and dysfunction. I wanted peace in my life. The only way to find it was to remove the toxic relationships.

Besides finding a job, my personal goal was to disconnect from Damenia, Chrissy and Nicki. I didn't want to need them anymore. I prayed for the understanding of why I needed them so much. I was hurt badly during the years. They abused and neglected by them. Their absence from my life scarred me. I didn't want to lose them again. The thought of being without them scared me. I missed and loved them so much. I would've dealt with or done just about anything to have and not lose them. But things were different. I wasn't a child, teenager or young adult. I was a thirty-five year old woman who needed to detach, and find my way without them. It was time for me to disconnect. They were killing me. They were the initial introduction to my abuse and uncertainties, and it was time to end.

I understood codependency as a mental condition where one person is controlled or manipulated by another who is mentally unstable or addicted to drugs. It also refers to the dependence on the needs of, or control of another. Sounds pretty unstable right? Well, that was me. I was completely locked into trying to save Chrissy, Damenia and Nicki. I was always excessively preoccupied with their problems and constantly placed a lower priority on my own needs. I always tried to make our relationship work and they never did. I always made plans to spend time with them or do something as a family. I always took them out or spent my money on them. I always assisted them with their birthday parties and they never helped, or offered me anything on my birthday. I was the only one putting energy into our relationships.

I felt tired, broken and lacked the strength I appeared to have. I destroyed myself for the sake of them. I didn't want to lose my family, but I realized if I wanted to better myself, walking away and distancing me from them was the way to go. They were all toxic. We were all toxic, but I had to find my way in life without them. I had to focus on me and stop trying to save them. I didn't have everything together not then or over the past 20 years, but I made a decision to separate myself from them.

They were all abusive and so was I. The difference was, I wanted better. I wanted different. I wanted to feel safe and not worry about threats and betrayal by Nicki, Chrissy and Demania anymore. Once I realized I was codependent, I focused on disconnecting. I asked myself what was I losing. I came up with many answers and none of them were good. I realized everything I needed to walk away from was negative. I was nowhere near perfect and had many flaws, dysfunctional behaviors and patterns, but I wanted freedom from it all.

I no longer wanted any broken or abusive relationships. From that moment, I focused on me. I protected Mama, but Chrissy, Nicki and Damenia were rocks under my shoes. For the next two months, it was all about finding a job and getting the hell away from them. I had enough. It was time for me to live for me, and stop dying for them. I sat in Mama's room and read the Bible many days seeking counsel and peace. Some days Nicki would come in and ask what I was doing. I always responded. *Reading the Bible* and nothing more. Nicki would stand there sometimes and look at me, and I kept my head in the Bible.

"What church is around here Mama?"
"Rhema Word."
"Where is that?"
"Not far. Do you want to go?
"I need to Mama."
That following Sunday, Mama and I got ready for church. I heard Damenia tell Nicki we were getting ready for church. I didn't want them to come.

"We're going to."

Damenia walked out of Nicki's room. I kept quiet, dressed myself and Shemar. I didn't see a reason to respond. I just had to get out of that house and work on me. I prayed for healing, understanding and a job. Attending church made my days a lot better in that house. Many Sundays after church we would come home and cook Sunday dinner. Mama was happy when we got along and weren't fighting. It was nice to enjoy my family when we were being rational. The next day, I had a job interview at Holy Cross Hospital. I felt really good about the job and had no doubts that it was mine. I came home from my job interview and went into Mama's bedroom.
"Hey Kelley."
"Hey."
"You never give up. I wish I had the same determination as you. Where do you get the strength from?"
"I guess it's in me. I can't give up. Just keep trying Nicki and things will get better."
I hugged Nicki and she cried. I understood her pain, but I had to stay focused on me. I refused to get caught up in her emotional drama again. I wanted out. Holy Cross hospital called me a few days after the interview, and the rest was history.

May 2006
I worked for Holy Cross for about four months before I found an apartment in Blue Island. Daniel went with me each time I had to view an apartment. Mama was sad, but I needed to leave, and start my life over. I thought maybe he wanted to tell me something throughout my disabled days. Many days I refuse to listen to His softly spoken works. I wanted to do things my way and if I hadn't sat down and listened, this day may have taken longer to arrive.

I didn't miss being in that house with Nicki and Damenia at all. I didn't have to worry about Chrissy because she never came to see Mama. Allen was missing in action as well. Make no mistake, we were all mentally unstable, but the difference between me and them was, I wanted peace and no more toxicity. I wanted difference and change. I was willing to do the work. I wanted to start over and raise my son away from all the noise and dysfunction. I didn't want him growing up around anything even remotely close to what I did. I wanted to better than my mother and someday a phenomenal wife. I wanted to remove the negativity and toxic relationships from my life. When I left things were better than before, but more drama and pain was right around the corner.

Mama's health was getting worse and no one seemed to care. She suffered with Hepatitis for over fifteen years and was constantly having biopsies of her liver. Everybody was so wrapped up in their own problems they didn't see what was coming. Nicki was the only one who helped me take care of Mama. We took Mama back and forth to her doctor's appointments, and made sure she took her medicine. I felt in my heart she wasn't getting better and began to concern myself with just how damaged Mama's liver was.

Taking My Power Back– 8

September 2006
At thirty-five years old, I started over in a very small two bedroom apartment in Blue Island. Daniel gave me two hundred dollars towards the apartment. It was nice and all the appliances were brand new. It was very small and when I say small, it was small. The kitchen was semi-connected to the living room, and on each side of the kitchen, was a bedroom. Right next to the bedroom and on the left side of the kitchen, was a bathroom. Connected to the living room was a large balcony covered with white vertical blinds, and brown carpet covered the floors.

I didn't have a bed or any other furniture. Mama let me borrow one of her televisions and purchased me a blow up bed. Daniel bought me two red, futon like circular chairs, and that was enough to get me started. I no longer liked him at all. I figured if he wanted to help, I'd let him. I didn't want him at all. I was still upset from what his mother did to Shemar. He was one person I really wanted out of my life, but having a kid with him prevented that.

November 2006
A few months after I moved in, Daniel wanted to have sex and during this gross interaction I told him to remove himself from me, and that was his last time touching me. I couldn't stand the thought of him touching me. I decided being friends was the best thing since we had a child together and Daniel agreed. I'm not certain if he believed me, but in time he had no choice but to accept it. We had a big argument and that lead to his confirmation.
"You're not taking my son anywhere with that damn attitude."
"I don't give a sh*t."
"As a matter of fact, you can get the f*ck out of my house."
"I don't give a f*ck."
"Give me my keys too you damn asshole."
"F*ck you, I don't give a sh*t about these keys b*tch."

Kelley Porter

"Your mama is a b*tch."
"I've been put out of worse places."
"Now your ass can get out of mine. Bye."
I slammed my door. Daniel had the nerves to try to dictate how I run my house, and I wasn't going for that. He was in for a rude awakening. I was stronger than before and since I stopped sleeping with him, he knew it was over. We argued and disrespected each other all the time. But after a while, Daniel and his mouth were complete history.

Some time passed and I realized I was still angry from all the pain Daniel caused me. I had to forgive him, but I was also accountable. Daniel was who he was before I met him and he had a history of manipulating, mistreating and cheating on women. I didn't have to stay, but since I did, I was just as responsible for being treated like garbage as he was for doing it. Men will only do what you allow them to do. No one placed a gun to my head and made me stay. I willingly stayed and for that, I am responsible. I stayed with him for seven years and as I mentioned before, I should have never gotten involved. But no sense in crying over spilled milk. I take responsibility.

At the very first sign of disrespect, abuse or disloyalty, I should have left. Daniel wasn't willing to correct his behaviors because he didn't see a problem. But I did and I stayed. He made a lot of mistakes, and did some cruel things to me, but I wreaked havoc on him just as well. Does that make him a bad person? Not really. But it does say he has many character defects, and some abnormal patterns and behaviors that needed attention. But that's neither here nor there. My goal was to forgive Daniel and myself. We were doing fine as parents, but I wanted to make certain there was complete closure.

"Hello."
"Hey Daniel."
"Hey, what's up?"
"If you're not busy, I need you to come by when you're free. I have a few things I'd like to talk to you about."

Mama was at my place relaxing as she had always been since I moved. I enjoyed her company and she made sure Shemar was okay when I went to work.

"Hey Granny."
"Hey Daniel, how are you doing?"
"I'm good. I'm good."
"How are you feeling?"
"A little tired, but I'm okay."
"So what's up Kelley?"
"Let's talk in the room. Daniel we have to maintain a respectful friendship for the sake of Shemar. We both did some terrible things to each other, but that's over now. The only way we're going to move forward is to leave what happened, behind us."
"Yea, you're right."
"You caused me a lot of pain, but I am accountable as well."
"For what?"
"First of all, I had no business dating you when I knew you had a woman. The moment Grace approached me, I should have walked away. I chose not to and for that I am responsible for a lot of the pain you caused me."
"I hear you, but that relationship was over a long time ago."
"Regardless, I should have never gotten involved with you. I would have never had to fight Grace if I never dated you."
"She was wrong for that."
"I'm not saying she was right, but I had no business coming in between you all. Not only that, after you gave me that STD, I should have left. I can think of many reasons why I should have never gotten involved with you as well as why I should have left you a long time ago, but that's not why I wanted to talk. The whole point of inviting you over was to tell you, I forgive you for all the pain you caused me. We need to respect each other so we can co-parent Shemar."
"I have no problem with that."
"There wasn't a lot of respect between us and I think we should try to do better now. There is no reason to disrespect

each other. I'm not dating you anymore, so things are different now."
"That's fine Kelley."
"If it's okay with you, I would like to take Shemar out as a family so he gets to spend time with us together. Your other kids are still welcome to come over."
"I wish my other baby mama's was like you."
"Daniel, I realize the only way I will get better is to admit my mistakes and learn from them. It doesn't make sense to keep talking about what you did because I didn't have to stay with you. So that's over now. I will respect your privacy and you need to respect mine."
"That sounds good. Thanks Kelley."
"You're welcome."
"Let me ride out. I have plans tonight."
"Okay. Enjoy yourself."
"See you later Granny."
"Take it easy Daniel."
"That sounds like that went well."
"It did Mama."
"I'm proud of you baby."
"Thanks Mama. I really don't have a problem with Daniel. I think he's still shocked I left him."
"He might be, but you did the right thing. I have to go back to the doctor on Thursday to have another Liver Biopsy and Nicki is taking me."
"Okay. What time? Do you need me to go with you?"
"No, just relax baby. You're doing enough. I will call you if I have any questions about what the doctor says. My appointment is at eleven o'clock."
"Okay, I'm tired Mama. I'm going to bed."
"Okay, I'm going to watch some TV."
"Good night Mama. I love you."
"Good night baby. I love you too."

January 2007
When I ceased sex with Daniel, I was no longer emotionally attached to him and that prevented him from hurting me

anymore. However, when I forgave him, I took all my power back. Daniel no longer controlled me. I forgave myself as well as Ms. Harris for hitting and leaving a bruise on Shemar's face. Now, that doesn't mean I like her or want anything to do with her.

After I broke up with and forgave Daniel, I was able to self-reflect. I wasn't able to see clearly where I went wrong while I was with him, but after I left, I learned my choices were poor. I had major character defects, dysfunctional patterns and behaviors. These are some of the things I learned about myself.

- Lack of self-love
- Low self-esteem
- Lack of confidence
- Cold and bitter heart
- Lack of knowledge about healthy a relationship
- Very disrespectful
- Abusive tongue
- I was still connected to sex in an unhealthy way
- I was not my authentic self
- I couldn't control my anger
- I lacked respect for men and women

Self-reflecting also led me to a better understanding of how poorly I behaved in my relationships with my family as well. Although I am the youngest and learned my unhealthy behaviors from them, I didn't have to behave irate, disrespectfully and like a victim. I was responsible for the toxic and abusive relationships in my life. As an adult, I made decisions that were not good for me and I had no one to blame but myself. If I was to really move forward and be a better woman, I had to reach back again and understand how badly and deeply the childhood abuse affected me. I had to do the work. It wasn't easy, but I did.

I worked on removing the toxic and unhealthy love I had for my family. I thought if I could conquer my instabilities, I would no longer be the emotionally unstable, dysfunctional and broken soul I was. I was partly right, but I was missing the most important thing.

March 2007
Nicki, me and a friend went out to Geno's. We had cocktails at home before leaving. Before we could even enjoy ourselves, Nicki had another cocktail and was more than drunk. She was ready to go home and we were not.
"I'm ready to go home."
"For real Nicki?"
"Yes. I'm drunk and ready to go home."
"Nicki can you just drink some water and sit down for a minute? We just got here. I'm not ready to go."
"I'm ready to go home."
"I'm not taking you home right now. I'm not ready to go."
"You need to take me home. I am drunk and I'm ready to go."
Nicki asked my friend and she refused at my request. I felt like Nicki should have just sat still and drank some water or she could have driven her own car. But I stood my ground and I didn't give a damn if she was mad.
"You f*cking bitch, take me the f*ck home now. Your ass is bogus. I'm ready to go."
"You should've driven your own damn car. You're the one who drank too damn much at home. Didn't nobody tell you to drink all that damn liquor."

Nicki continued to cuss and snap on the patio of Geno's in front of many people. I ignored her and eventually she left. She walked home and it actually felt good to stand up to her and not worry about seeing her again. As time passed, I got better and better. I no longer wanted my family as I did in the past. My fear of losing them was decreasing as well.

In the past, I would have caved into the verbal arguments or bullying. For the sake of saving my relationship with Nicki, I would have done just about anything. I felt good about myself, but there was more to come. I had a party at my place and Nicki refused to respect my wishes.

"I asked you not to bring Damenia over my house."
"You need to stop that. We're family."
"Guess what, ain't neither one of y'all asses coming in."
This b*tch just don't have no respect. I bet she won't do that shit again. I thought. I closed my door and walked to the kitchen. After that day, Nicki stopped bringing Damenia to my house.
My phone rang.
"Hello."
"Why don't you want me in your house?"
Damenia called to question me.
"Because your ass uses drugs and I don't want that around me or my son."
I hung the phone up. Nicki let her use the phone like that was going to change something. I learned so much about her during this last year and none of it was pretty. She was an instigator, fickle as hell and couldn't be trusted. Nicki proved to me time after time she was as deceitful and disrespectful as Damenia, and Chrissy was. I refused to believe who she exposed to me. From that day forward, Nicki started to be very manipulative. Whenever I invited her over, she always told me she had Damenia with her. I never caved in to that mess. After the mess Nicki did at Mama's house, she was lucky I allowed her back in my house.

Nicki and I were the closest among us all, or so I thought. Daniel always said she was jealous of me, but I never believed him. I confided in him a lot about some of the things she did to me and his conclusion was that she was jealous. I always knew Chrissy was, but to see Nicki in that way was difficult for me. My entire life I wanted acceptance from Chrissy, peace from Damenia and now I just didn't want to lose Nicki. I really wanted my family, but so much time had passed and too much bad blood was between us. The best thing for me to do was to walk away and redefine myself without them. Many days I cried because I wanted my family. I missed the relationship I wanted so badly with them. I feared losing them again, but I wasn't afraid to lose the unhealthy and toxic relationships we had.

I was still very emotionally attached to all of them and hated it; all that meant for me was more pain. I wanted to get to a point where if I didn't see them it wasn't a bother; if they didn't want to go out with me, it wasn't a bother. I just wanted to learn to stand in my truth with or without them. I had to take my power back. Being in my place gave me a sense of freedom and happiness, but in the back of my mind, I really wanted a decent relationship with Nicki. It didn't matter if Damenia came to visit. Her drug use became a thorn in my ass and I was over her. I didn't care if Chrissy visited. I just wanted her to stop criticizing and show me some love. She never did, but I learned to accept that and move forward.

It took me another four years to gain my full power back. But I did. I no longer need them to live. I no longer need to see them every day. I no longer need to talk to them every day. I love my family, but my life is more peaceful without them. Sometimes what's good for you, will kill you. I am free from the toxic relationships I had with all of them including Daniel. I have no regrets today, but life is far better when you remove the negativity and toxicity from your lives. I am free.

April 2007
I moved into one of the larger units and fully furnished it. I did well at work, and Shemar played baseball for our local kids team. He attended Paul Revere Primary school and met new friends in kindergarten. Mama was at my place. I didn't mind her being there

as long as she was away from the drama. She was sick and things did not seem to get better. Nicki took Mama to the doctor and the results shocked all of us. After eighteen years of having Hepatitis C, Mama's doctor diagnosed her with liver cancer. I called everyone in the family and just as they were on their way to my place, I received a phone call.

"Hey Kelley, this is your cousin D. I need you to tell your mother, granddaddy died; her father died."

"What? Granddaddy died. What happened?"

"I can give you the details later, but now I need to call everybody.

"Okay. Thanks."

I hadn't even processed the information about Mama having Cancer and now if things couldn't get worse. I was just informed she had Cancer and now I had to tell her about her father passing away. She was on her way to my place with Nicki, and I didn't want to tell her, but I had to. I wanted to wait until she made it to my place, but something told me to call her while she was with Nicki.

The phone rang.
"Hello."
"Hey Mama, I need to tell you something."
"What's wrong baby girl?"
"Your father passed."
"Say what? What did you say baby?"
"Granddaddy died. Your father died."
"Aw naw Kelley, naw."
Cries from Mama's voice pierced a hole straight through my heart. I cried with her. I hated to see or hear Mama cry.
"What happened? Who called?"
Mama cried.
"Cousin D called Mama. She said she would fill us in when we get to grandma's house."
"Oh my God, why, why, why?"
"Mama, please stop crying. It's going to be okay. Come home Mama, and then we will go to your mother's house."
"Okay, baby. I'll tell Nicki."

Mama having cancer devastated me. Although granddaddy died, it didn't hit me as hard because I didn't have a strong relationship with him. I was more so hurt for my mother. She loved her father and now she had to deal with two heartaches in one day. By the time we made it to Grandma's house, everybody was there and honestly I was more concerned with Mama's health. I would've preferred to take her home and let her rest. But he was her stepfather, and I understood.

The next few weeks were very depressing for Mama. She had too much to deal with, and I tried to keep her happy. Cancer was more than she could handle.
"Kelley what's going to happen to me?"
"Mama you're going to be fine. The doctors will put you on the transplant list and the University of Chicago is good at these things. I've seen them save many patients who needed a liver."
Although I tried to make Mama feel better, I had a bad feeling about the situation. I said whatever I could to keep Mama's mindset free of worry.

May 2007
"Mama everything is going to be okay. Chemotherapy is used all the time to treat patients with cancer. This will be easy. So don't worry."
"Okay baby."
Mama was afraid.
"Good morning Ms. Porter and Kelley."
"Good morning doctor."
We both spoke at the same time.
"Today we're going to do the Chemotherapy treatment and radiation. The purpose is to shrink the liver tumors. But we can't radiate the tumor on the upper part of your liver. It's too close to your heart."
"So what does that mean doctor?"
"Your mother will have to go on the Liver Transplant list."
"Okay, is it okay if we, her children get tested for compatibility?"

"I don't think it will be a good idea for you because you are your mother's caregiver, and we will need you. But you can ask everyone else."
"Okay, I understand."
"We're going to get your mother ready and you can wait if you want or leave, and come back."
"Okay, Mama don't worry. This is easy and I will be right here waiting for you. I love you."
"I love you too baby."
"See you in a little while. Thanks doctor."

I waited in the outpatient area for Mama. I wasn't really concerned about the chemotherapy or radiation treatment. I worked on the Oncology unit for three and half years, so I've seen the effects of chemotherapy. But this therapy was somewhat different. It was localized to her liver. I was afraid for Mama especially after the doctor confirmed she would be placed on the transplant list. I've seen many patients wait months for a liver and die, and others took the color of a banana. This was a very trying for me and my family. I called everyone to tell them about the compatibility testing. No one went to get tested and others were not a good donor. This really broke my heart. I would've given Mama any organ if it would've saved her life. The thought of donating your only liver scared everyone as the recovery process was a lengthy one, so I understood why no one went to get tested.

The procedure was complete and the doctor discharged Mama. She was in pain so I took her to my house so she could recover without any stress. I bathed and combed her hair. I maintained my courage and didn't show any fear or sadness around Mama. About a week later Mama fully recovered and wanted to go by her place. I convinced Mama to stay at my place and relax while I went by her house to pick up clothing. When I got there, I talked with Nicki and Damenia about the seriousness of Mama's condition.

"Y'all need to get it together. Mama won't live forever."

"Mama ain't going no damn where."
Damenia took Mama for granted.
"Where is Mama at?"
"Nicki she's at my place. I just came to pick up some of her stuff."
"I miss her. When is she coming back?"
"Call her. She doesn't want to be here Nicki."

I knew Nicki cared, but Damenia didn't seem to care. I picked up Mama's clothing and went back to my place. I didn't want Mama around Nicki or Damenia. They were selfish, disrespectful and full of themselves. Damenia was certain Mama would always be around, and she would be able to live with her. They were comfortable living with Mama and had no idea their days had come to an end in that house. They never tried to get their lives in order, especially Damenia. I knew in my heart something wasn't right.

July 2007
"Hello."
"Hi, is this Kelley?"
"Yes, it is."
"This is Jennifer, Dr. Mardin's nurse. We found your mother a liver and we wanted to schedule her for surgery."
"Excellent."
"But before we do, she will have to come in for pre-op testing."
"Do you want me to run the test on Mama?"
Over the years, I drew Mama's blood and tested it at work to save time. I kept an eye on her glucose and liver function level. Her doctors at the University of Chicago knew I worked in the lab so they were okay with that.
"Not this time Kelley. We have to do our own pre-op testing."
"Okay. When is the surgery?"
"We scheduled your mom's surgery for Wednesday, July twenty-fifth. We need you to bring your mother in a day before for her blood work."
"Okay."
"Thanks Kelley. We will see you then."

I called the family and told them the good news and everybody was very happy.

August 25th, 2007

"Mama, it's time."
"I'm getting up now."
Shemar stayed overnight with Daniel so I could take Mama to the hospital and be there when she awoke. I called Nicki and Damenia so they could get ready. Chrissy and Allen were awake. We went to the hospital and prayed for Mama's return.

"Ok everybody we have to get your mother ready for surgery."

The nurse took Mama to surgery. I saw the fear in Mama's eyes. We were all scared. Chrissy, Nicki and Damenia cried. I know Mama trusted my feelings so I had to make her feel comfortable and sure so I never cried. I was scared sh*tless for Mama. I stayed strong for her. Everybody said their last words and my last words to Mama was *I love you and see you later.*

We waited four to six hours, and finally the nurse took Mama to the Intensive Care Unit. Within the next twenty four hours, mama needed a second surgery and the following two days were something unbelievable.

Mama had tubes coming from every hole in her body; a heart monitor, pulse oximeter, intubated and, on life support. For forty-eight hours, I watched Mama lie there lifeless in that bed. The room appeared brighter than any other hospital room. Mama was completely covered in white sheets up to her neck. She had a tube in her mouth and nose. Her stomach was connected to a Jackson Pratt tube and the container filled with bright red blood. Her eyes pried open with tape, and the nurses insisted we did not touch her. The cardiac monitor signaled Atrial Fibrillation and her pulse was question mark/seventy.

Her eyes were lifeless. I knew in my heart mama was dead and instead of the doctors being honest, they kept my mother in that bed until seventy hours expired, and then called a "Dr. Cart;" meaning CPR and defibrillator needed. I know they made a deadly mistake in surgery. I also know when a patient comes into the emergency room; or admitted for surgery, and dies within seventy hours, the body is automatically examined by the Cook County coroner. Those doctors thought we were some dumb black folks. I beg to differ. My fifteen years in healthcare and degrees taught me so much more. I knew something wasn't right when the heart monitor signaled Atrial Fibrillation and looking into her lifeless eyes.

August 28th, 2007
"Is she dead? Is she dead!?"
I punched Dr. Perry on his arm.
"No, but she will be here for a while."

I left the hospital to get food and in the process of returning, I heard the overhead page "Dr. Cart" being called and it was in Mama's room. I ran through the hospital as fast as I could to the elevator. When I made it to Mama's room, the doctors were performing CPR on her. I watched in agony as tears rolled down my face. Six health care providers crowded Mama's bed. Her small body being compressed on as the one of the doctors yelled "*CLEAR*;" they shocked Mama's body and after what seemed like forever, they stopped. Dr. Ann walked over to me.
"I'm sorry Kelley. We did all we could do, but we couldn't save her."
"No, No, No, No, No!"
I fell to the floor. I sat there with my knees to my chest and sobbed like a baby.
"Kelley, what would you like for us to write as the cause of death?"
"Why are you asking me? You should know?"

That question alone with every unusual act I noticed while Mama laid in that bed sparked something in me and my Aunt. I decided to have Mama's body removed from the University of Chicago hospital and have the autopsy performed elsewhere. I filed a wrongful death, malpractice lawsuit and won. It didn't bring Mama back, but I needed those doctors and the hospital held accountable for their negligence and they were. Mama is gone and the thought of it makes me want to cry. I miss Mama. She was my angel. I loved her so much. But, I know she's at peace now.

Mama's death took a toll on me. I gained fifteen pounds and was completely in denial. I needed Mama, but she was no longer with me. The pain I felt from her death could've easily led to depression. I wasn't myself afterwards and allowed more pain and stress to fill my heart. All the hard work I did to regain my power, and I felt like I lost my soul when mama died.

December 2007
As of December thirty-first your employment at Holy Cross Hospital will be terminated.

I opened a piece of mail addressed from Holy Cross Hospital and learned of my termination while off work due to a work injury. I was somewhat upset, but I really didn't care. Mama was gone and I received worker's compensation benefits. Like the death of Mama wasn't enough pain to put me under. I thought it couldn't get any worse. I was wrong.

I was very sad and lonely, and felt like I needed something or someone. I met a gentleman named Mark at Wal-Mart. When I looked at him, I thought he was very fine. More so of what folks called men "pretty boy" when they were too cute to be a male. Mark was mixed with Puerto Rican.

He was about six feet two inches; very light skin, curly hair, very thin build, green eyes and a very pretty smile. He wasn't my type. I preferred dark skinned men with a medium, athletic build, but since I only lusted for him, it was no big deal. Mark pushed a buggy with a small white child in it and I bumped into him several times. *If I bump into him one more time I'm going to say something. It looks like the mother of his child is a white woman. Oh well, f*ck her.* I thought. I did. I walked pass him in the linen aisle and the rest was worse than any relationship I ever had.

"You are one fine man with beautiful eyes."
"Thank you shorty."
Mark smiled.
"You're thick as hell."
"Write your phone number down. I take it your woman is somewhere nearby so I will step over there."
"My girl, in fact, write yours down."
"Okay."

I wrote my phone number down and days later, Mark called me. He and his girlfriend Candy lived together in his sister's building. Mark complained about not wanting Candy any more just like Daniel complained about Grace. He painted a clear and pretty picture of himself and not long after, I discovered he was another lying, abusive male I fell for. I saw signs in the very beginning. Nevertheless, like Daniel, I was going to fix Mark.

The Power of Self-Love – 9

January 2008

The ground was covered with at least four inches of snow, and plenty of ice beneath it; there were mountains of snow pushed to the sides of the streets and everyone drove about fifteen miles per hour.

"Where are we?"

"Just get out the car."

"Why?"

"Get the f*ck out of the car!"

"For what? If you're just running in, I can sit here and wait."

Mark angrily jumped out of the car and walked over to the passenger side. My eyes followed him along the front end of the car. He staggered and his eyes looked like the devil possessed him.

"What the f*ck are you doing?"

I held on the steering wheel.

"Get out of the damn car!"

"Why?! It's too damn cold outside."

"Stop f*cking grabbing me. What the hell is wrong with you?"

Mark staggered to his friend's house and knocked on the door. He stood there in four inches of snow waiting for someone to answer. It was dark, very cold and there was no reason for me to stand outside with him. Mark got back in the car and started it up.

"Don't ever put your hands on me. There was no reason for you to try to pull me out of this car. That sh*t was unnecessary. I don't believe in fighting men and I sure as hell don't believe in being hit by one."

Mark pulled off and slowly drove into the night as his tires slid left and right on the snowy pavement. Only two weeks after I met him, he proved he was an abusive and unstable man. A few days after, Mark called.

"Hello."

"Hey Kelley."

"Hey Mark."

"I'm leaving Candy. She's too damn nasty and every time I come home, her male friend is over here. She said he's been her best friend for a long time."
"Is it okay with you for her to have a man in your house while you're not home?"
"Hell naw."
"How old is she? She should know better."
"She's nineteen."
"Nineteen and you're going on thirty-six. Why are you dating someone so young? She's way too young for you."
"I like them young. I met her at Apple Bee's two years ago when I was the head chef and one thing led to another."
"Really, that doesn't even sound right. One year younger and you would've been a child molester."
"Well, I'm not."
"You should have never gotten involved with her."
"When she got pregnant, and I believe on purpose, I moved to Indiana so I could be close to her. I tried to do the right thing, but her parents hated me."
"I would too if you were messing with my teenage daughter and you're a grown ass man. You should've known better."
"She's on her way in the house, so I will call you later."

What the hell? What grown ass man dates a teenager and gets her pregnant? Another trifling ass nigga like Daniel. What a damn waste. What is wrong with men today? He is a controlling nigga and he got the wrong one because that sh*t ain't even happening. I have been through enough sh*t and I am not taking any more from any man. I thought.

February 2008
I told Mark he could stay with me while he saved his money. He wanted to leave his sister's building because she was a slumlord. Mark and I planned on being together.
My phone rang.
"Hello."
"Hey Kelley, I packed all of her belongings and she's leaving now."
"Does she know you're on the phone?"

"Naw, I'm in the other room. She's mad as hell. We got into a big argument and I don't care, because like you said she's too damn young for me. We ain't going anywhere."
"Call me when you're done."
"Okay."

It was about eight o'clock in the morning and very cold outside. I could feel the wind creeping in from the small crack in my bedroom window. I didn't have a storm window and it was somewhat off track, making room for that hawk to ease in. This was one cold day.

"Hello."
"Hey Kelley."
"Hey Mark."
"She left and I'm at work now so why don't you come by tomorrow. "That's cool."
"Okay. See you tomorrow."

Why am I dealing with this dude? He ain't my type. This is no different from Daniel. I thought.

Mark evicted his two-year old child and her mother. What type of man does something like that in the middle of the winter? The man I wanted. I was out of my mind to think things would work between him and me. He was a horrible man from the beginning, and to think I was any better for pressuring him to put Candy out. I was worse than he was. I constantly told Mark he needed to put Candy out, and never once thought about her or their child. I agreed with and egged him on every single time he spoke poorly of her, or talked about putting her out. I knew it was wrong and I didn't care. I wanted what I wanted and I didn't care who got hurt, but the tables turned on me later, and I must say Karma is a b*tch.

The next day I drove to Mark's place. I looked in the refrigerator and thought, *how nasty.* I added to his criticism about Candy. There wasn't much left in his place, except a kitchen table, a couch and some clothing. *Finally, he's mine.* I thought. A few days later Mark moved into my place, but we had an arrangement.

"You can stay here for two months and that is enough time for you to save your money, and find a place to live."

"That's cool. Thank you."

Mark slept on the couch in the living room for the most part and some days he would sneak into my bedroom while Shemar was asleep. I didn't allow him to interact with Shemar. Not to mention, Shemar was mostly with his father or in school. A week after Mark moved in, and on a Friday evening at about four o'clock, Mark came home from work and I was completely insulted by what I saw.

"Don't come in my damn house drunk like that. You could've stayed wherever the hell you were. That doesn't make any damn sense."

"I'm not bothering you so why does it matter if I'm drunk? I'm not drunk."

"Tell that lie to somebody who was born yesterday. I don't want this sh*t around my son. Now if you must get that damn drunk when you go out, don't come back to my house."

"That's fine."

Mark had this dumb look on his face. He left the house and didn't come back until the next morning. I was furious and not necessarily at him, but at myself for allowing a man I didn't really know in my house, and around my kid. Shemar was six years old and Lord knows I never wanted him around an alcoholic. Mark reminded me of my alcoholic brother and I hated every moment of it. *What the hell was I thinking? How could I allow any man to move into my place, and around my damn son? I am one desperate ass female. He's a damn alcoholic and I will never leave my baby with him. I should have never let him move in. That was just damn dumb.* I thought.

Mark decided to respect my wishes and save his drinking for the weekend. If he decided to drink, he didn't come to my place and I was okay with that. I cannot and will not tolerate alcoholics and addicts. I didn't understand how this man made such money and didn't have a car, cell phone, no winter boots or a coat. He was a diesel mechanic and had the means.

There was a knock at my door.

"Who is it?"

"Mark."

I opened the door and he smelled like a liquor factory. I could smell the old liquor reeking from his pores.

"Ugh. You stink. I hope you had fun."

"I did until I had to sleep in my car in this cold ass weather."

"You're the one who chose to get drunk out of your damn mind. I don't want that mess around me."

"I'm going to take a shower."

"Do you have plans tonight?"

"No. Why?"

"I'm going to Genos and if you want to come, you can."

"What's Genos, and where is it?"

"It's a sports bar in Calumet Park, down the street from here. I've been going there for years and it's very nice."

"Yea, that's cool. What about your son?"

"Shemar is spending the weekend with his father."

"What's your baby daddy name again?"

"Do you mean son's father?"

"Whatever Kelley."

"His name is Daniel."

"That's good you don't have a problem with him spending time with his son."

"Why should I? That's his father and if any man tries to come between our friendship or has a problem with him visiting his son, their ass is history."

"I hear you. Since I left Candy she refuses to let me see my daughter. I know her parents got something to do with it. She's mad because I'm living here, and said she doesn't want our daughter around another female, but she has my daughter around her guy friends."

"She sounds bitter to me."

"She's can't keep my daughter away for too long."

Mark came out of the shower and wanted me to join him in the bedroom.

"This is what I'm going to do to you when you act up."

Mark tried to pound on me and having a well-endowed penis, it was very painful. He had no remorse. I locked my thighs around his legs and prevented him from hurting me any longer. His sex was very rough, abusive and painful. That was another sign of him being an abusive man and I should've put him out of my place. Later that night, we went to Genos. Since everyone knew me, the first fifteen minutes consisted of me hugging and chatting with all the men, and women I knew.

"I don't want you to hug and let all these niggas kiss on you."

"Boy please, these guys are my friends and they will be here when you're gone."

"Yea, okay."

"You act like their kissing me on my mouth. I've known these men before Shemar was born and when we haven't seen each other in a while that's how we greet each other. Now if you think you're going to control me, you may as well let that go now because it ain't going to happen."

"I'm not trying to control you. You can have some respect. What if my female friends hugged and kissed me on the cheek?"

"If they're your friends, then it's not a problem."

"Yea, we will see."

"I'm going to get a cocktail and I'm done with this conversation."

Mark and I decided to have a few cocktails and dance a bit. I introduced Mark to my guy friends and we continued to chat, dance, and drink. After a long island and a half, I had enough. I was ready to go home. I drove home because Mark was completely wasted. We made it home and Mark tried to have sex with me, but I refused.

"Why are you telling me no?"

"Because I'm drunk and have no control. So if you don't mind waiting until the morning."

"I will just jag off."

"Go ahead."

I didn't believe Mark was going to jag off. He did, and as time went by, I realized that was an ongoing thing for him.

"I'm going to bed."

Mark continued to satisfy himself and I really didn't care. I refuse to have sex while being drunk. I felt like he would take advantage and pound even harder. By morning, the phone rang.

"Hello."

"Hey Kelley, I'm on my way with baby Mar."

"Okay."

It was about eight o'clock in the morning and Shemar was on his way home. I never wanted Shemar to see any man in my room. My personal life was off-limits to my son. I never wanted him to grow up and think his Mama was a whore.

"You have to put some clothes on and go in the front. My son is on his way home."

"Why do I have to leave your room? Can't you just close the door?" "Nope, I don't want my son to see any men in my bedroom."

"He saw his father in here."

"Key word; father—now go in the living room."

"If I didn't know any better, I would think you were still f*cking him."

"Think what you want to, but you still have to go in the living room."

"Is Daniel coming inside?"

"Yep, why?"

What the hell type of question was that. I thought.

"Why is he coming in?"

"That's my damn son's father and if you plan on trying to reject him that means you reject my son and I'm not having that sh*t. You can go in the damn bathroom."

Mark dressed himself slowly, and I knew when Daniel said he was on his way, he was usually around the corner. I refused to have my son come home and see any man walking around half-dressed, or in my bedroom. I felt that was a lack of respect for my son. If anyone was going to disrespect my son,

it would be me and not some man. Mark looked at me with this crazy look and went into the bathroom.
"Who is it?"
"It's us."
"Hey Kelley."
I bent over, hugged and kissed Shemar.
"Hey Mommy."
The sound of his kind little voice always made my heart melt.
"I'm sorry. I didn't know you had company."
"Daniel, you can still come in."
"Mark, this is Daniel. Daniel this is Mark."
"Hey, how are you doing?"
"What's up Daniel? It's nice to meet you."
I'm thinking, *this lying phony b*tch ass nigga. A few minutes ago you had a problem with him coming in. Phony ass punk.*
"Likewise, Kelley I'm not going to stay long. I just wanted to bring Shemar up and holler for a minute."
"That's cool."
"Did he eat?"
"Yea. I just fed him, so he's good."
Daniel and I chatted about Mama's death and Mark sat on the couch in silence.
"If you need me to take him to school in the morning just call me."
"Alright."
"Shemar come say bye to your father."
"Bye Dad. I love you."
"I love you too baby Mar."

Later that night, I put Shemar to bed and decided to clean my kitchen as I always did before I went to bed. Mark sat on my double recliner, tan, leather couch with the recliner extended. I removed the white garbage bag from my garbage can and before I could tie the string around it, Mark decided he had a few words to say.
"Why don't you put that sh*t down and come over here."
"I'm cleaning my kitchen and you can feel free to help."
"Naw, that ain't even necessary. Can't that wait till tomorrow?"

"No, you can wait till tomorrow. I do things the way I do and if you don't like it, too damn bad. If your ass wanted to spend some time you could've been nicer so after I'm done, I'm going to bed."

*Who the hell does he think he is trying to tell me when to clean my house up? He ain't running sh*t up in here. Stupid, alcoholic bastard.* I thought as I walked toward my bedroom.

A few days later, Mark and I went out to have cocktails and then stopped by Chrissy's place. We pulled up outside and parked the car.
"I'm not going in."
"Then why did we come down here?"
"Go upstairs and do what you have to do, and I will just wait."
"We're visiting, not just me."
"That's your damn family not mines. So go ahead before I put you out my f*cking car."
"What the hell is wrong with you?"
"You don't even talk about your mama."
"What the hell does my mother have to do with this? I don't talk about her because I choose not to. Why do I need to talk to you about my mother?"
"Kelley you can get the f*ck out my car and find a way home."
"I'm not getting out of sh*t. Why the f*ck did you even bother t come out if you were going to act like this. Drunk ass, now you wanna start some shit."
"I'm not drunk. I'm just sick of your ass."
"You can't be sick of me. Be sick of your own ass. I ain't done sh*t to you. Now please take me home."

Snow covered the ground, and I refused to spend a night at Chrissy's place. I humbled myself and politely asked Mark to take me home.

"Mark, will you please take me home? I really don't know what's wrong with you, but we were to have a good time tonight. So if you have changed your mind, that is fine with me."

Mark started the car and pulled off. *Thank goodness.* I thought. The entire ride was in silence until we came close to home.
"Are you coming back out?"
"I'm not sure. Why?"
"Because I'm going to hang out with my boy, but I will be back."
"Just call me if I'm not at home."
"A'ight. That's fine."
It was only six o'clock in the evening and I knew I was going to leave back out. I was dressed and ready to party. I didn't see a need to tell him I was going back outside. Mark pulled off and I went to Genos as I always did. I wasn't too particular about bar hopping or visiting the many clubs as I had in the past. Genos was like home to me and everybody knew me.
"Hey Kels, what are you drinking girl?!"
One of the bartenders greeted me.
"Ciroc, and Cranberry."
"No Long Island?!"
"Not tonight girl. Take my coat."
"Hand it over the bar."
I was ready to dance. Stepping was my favorite type of dance, and over the years I had gotten so much better. The night was moving along just fine and I enjoyed myself with my friends.
"Kels, what are you doing with that light-skinned ass nigga? He's a damn punk and I know he ain't your type."
My friend Thomas didn't like Mark. I never knew why, but I guess he saw something I didn't.
"You're right about that. He's just something to do. Nigga insecure and jealous as hell."
"You should've got with a real nigga like me."
"Thomas you're my boy and you know that ain't happening."
"Damn, diss me like that."
"Man, stop it."
"Come on dance with me."
Thomas extended his hand toward me.
"Let's do it."

We stepped to at least four songs and I loved it. Thomas dipped and spun me from the left to the right. We waltzed and I followed his every move.

"Kels, look who's standing at the door."

"No this nigga didn't."

I waved and gave Mark the wait a second finger.

"Did you know he was coming up here?"

"Hell no."

"Wow, stalking ass punk. That's a b*tch move."

Thomas turned me into his arms and I could tell that made Mark angry. I looked towards the door and Mark was standing there watching while I danced with Thomas. Eventually the song ended, and I walked over to him.

"Hey, what are you doing up here?"

"I stopped by the crib and you weren't there so I figured you would be up here. Then I called your phone and you didn't answer."

"My phone is in my purse."

"Why was that nigga hugging and dipping you like that? I know that's your boy and all, but don't you think that's too much?"

"Nope, that's a part of stepping. Maybe you should learn."

"That sh*t didn't even look right."

"I'm not doing this with you so if you wanna hang and dance, that's cool. But if you think you're going to ruin my night, it's not going to happen."

"I will have one drink and I'm leaving. Are you leaving with me?"

"Nope. I've only been here a couple of hours and the earliest I'm leaving is midnight or one o'clock."

"What the f*ck you gotta be out 'til one for. Unless you're looking to f*ck somebody, I don't see the point."

"I do not have time for this sh*t."

I walked out of Mark's face and continued to enjoy myself. He watched me and flirted with other women. I guess he was trying to get a response out of me, but it didn't work. I talked to my boys as I always did, and didn't miss one beat.

"I'm leaving now. Are you coming with me?"

"No. I'm not ready to go."

"Whatever. I'm out."
This Negro has lost his damn mind if he thinks he's going to control me. He better go and find a young chick that ain't smart enough to know the difference. I thought.
I continued to party until about one o'clock in the morning. I cut myself off after two or three drinks because I didn't want to drive home wasted. When I made it home, Mark wasn't there and I was glad because Lord knows I didn't want his drunken attitude around me. I looked at the clock and it was about three o'clock in the morning. There was a knock at my door. I opened the door and Mark staggered right past me and into the bathroom.
"Can I come in the room with you?"
"I'm tired and I'm going back to sleep."

March 2008
"Have you been saving your money because you only have thirty more days left here?"
"Yep, I've been saving so I'm good."
"Okay, great."
My telephone rang.
"Hello."
"Hey Daniel, what's up?"
"Nothing much; just being nosy. What's up with Mark?"
"Sh*t. He's saving his money so he can find his own place. He was living with his girlfriend in his sister's building. He put her out and is now looking for his own place."
"Kelley you better be careful with that nigga. Any man who leaves his own place for a woman after a few months of knowing her, is unstable. He better not f*ck with my son."
"You ain't even got to worry about that one. He ain't crazy. He might be insecure and jealous, but the nigga ain't crazy enough to mess with mine. I never leave Shemar alone with him anyway. We're not a couple. He sleeps on the couch. He's a nice guy until his ass drinks."
"Oh, one of those."
"But guess what; his ass sleeps in the car or somewhere else when he's drunk. I don't let him in."
"That's cold as hell."

"Yep, and the outside is as well."
Daniel and I laughed.
"Kelley!" Mark yelled from the living room.
"What?!"
"What are you doing?!"
"I'm on the phone with Daniel!"
"Don't tell that nigga you're on the phone with me."
"Why not? You're my son's father and I can talk to you."
"Oh, when you're done, I need to holler at you."
"Kelley I will talk to you later."
"We ain't got to get off the phone."
"You go holler at that nigga. I will call you later."
Daniel and I became closer as friends. We chatted on the phone constantly and shared our problems with each other.
"What's up Mark?"
"The way you and Daniel are always on the phone, are you sure you're not f*cking him?"
"I don't have time for this insecure ass sh*t. Just because you and your daughter's mother aren't talking doesn't mean I can't talk with my son's father."
"I'm not insecure."
"The hell you aren't and in fact, you may as well be quiet because I'm not arguing with you."
*This mother*cker has lost his mind. Insecure bum ass. If he thinks he's going to stop me from talking to Daniel, he can think again.* I thought.

Some days when Mark wasn't being as insecure jerk, we had fun. But for the most part, I didn't like him and wanted him the hell out of my place. The next few weeks felt like they were moving very slow, and the winter didn't help. Mark came home from work with a certain behavior that I was all too familiar with.
"Hey." Mark skipped and hopped down my hallway with this huge smile on his face.
"What's wrong with you? Why all the excitement and being hyper?"
"I'm just happy to see you."
"Oh, look like you had something."

"Had what? I don't mess with coke anymore and I hope you don't hold that against me. I told you I haven't used in five years."
"Okay, you're just a little too hyper for me."
"That ain't it. Can I just be happy?"
"You sure can and I hope it's not drugs."
We were both silent as we put the groceries away Mark purchased. I was certain Mark smoked some crack or sniffed some cocaine. I couldn't quite place my finger on it, but my gut feeling told me he was high off cocaine. Shemar wasn't home so Mark decided to go in my room and watch television.
"Kelley, if I asked you to pop some pills with me, would you do it?"
"Pills, hell no, drugs; you are out of your damn mind and if you ever ask me about that sh*t again, not only will I put your ass out, but I will stop f*cking with you."
"I was just asking. A couple of my ex-women popped ecstasy with me."
"That's them and I don't use any drug unless it's prescription."
"I'm not going to ask you anymore."
"I'm far from stupid. You must still use for you to ask me that sh*t."
"Naw, I quit five years ago, but I did pop some ecstasy here and there with my baby mama, and the women before her."
"I don't f*ck around."
"I hear you." *This nigga got me f*cked up with some young, dumb bitch. Ain't no sober or drug free nigga gonna ask some sh*t like that. I want this nigga out of my crib. His ass is probably still uses cocaine and I wonder if I talked to his baby mama, would she know? The truth always comes out.* I thought.

April 2008
"Kelley you can just take me to my mom's house?"
Mark packed his clothing.
"I take it you don't have money for an apartment."
"Not enough, I need one more month."

"Naw, you had two months and that should've been enough. You only gave me two hundred dollars a month and bought food."

"It's cool."

I know his ass didn't think he was going to live with me another day. He has to get the hell out of my place. Good riddance. I thought.

May 2008

The sun was shining, the flowers were blooming and the smell of summer was right around the corner. Almost a year passed since Mama died and I moved along pretty well. I missed and needed her greatly. Daniel kept Shemar more than often. Shemar was in Martial Arts, swimming lessons and playing baseball. He was happy and so was I. I missed Mark and now and then, I talked to him. But I knew he wasn't right for me or my son. Mr. Mark was worse off than I thought he was and be ready because this man is like many walking the streets today so pay attention.

"Hello."

"Hey Kelley."

"What's up Mark? How are you?"

"I'm good. I think I found an apartment, but I just need proof of income. Do you mind taking me to my boy's shop so I can pick up some paperwork?"

"Yea, that's cool. Can you come now?"

"Give me thirty minutes."

I was happy Mark found a place to stay. I didn't know where at that time, but I found out later.

"Thanks Kelley, I appreciate this."

"You're welcome. So where is your apartment?"

"I'm trying to get in your complex, but I just have to give some more paperwork."

"Really."

"Yep, I really don't want to stay in the city and it seems nice out by you."

"It's quiet. Sometimes you don't even hear a dog bark."

Mark picked up the paperwork he needed and I dropped him back off at his mother's house. We didn't talk every day. But the line of communication stayed open. A week later, Mark called.
"Hello."
"Hey Kelley. I got an apartment."
"Where at?"
"On your block."
"On my block?"
"Yep, in the A building. Come to the back."
"Okay."
I walked out the back entrance of my building and toward the 'A' building and he was moving his items in. I was somewhat shocked, but I didn't think much of it. I helped Mark get started. I went to Walmart and bought him a reddish bowl and cup set, silverware and dish towels. I still didn't consider him a boyfriend, but I didn't mind buying him a few items for his apartment.
"I have to go now. I'm about to do laundry."
"Maybe I can stop by later."
"Yea that's cool."
Shemar was with Daniel and stayed for a few weeks during the summer. I was still off work, receiving unemployment, but actively seeking a job.
"Hello."
"Hey Kelley."
"Hey Daniel, what's happening?"
"Nothing much, just calling to chat."
"Ok, hold on. Let me take my coat off and get situated."
"I'm back."
"Why this damn female gets drunk and become paranoid? She starts talking about marriage and who the f*ck I slept with. I'm like we ain't no damn couple."
"She sounds like Mark. Maybe their asses should date."
"Why this nigga move in down the street?"
"Down the street from where?"
"From me."

"Get the f*ck out of here. Kelley, I told you that nigga was crazy. That's f*cked up. Sh*t. I thought this girl was crazy. Kelley, stay away from his ass."
"Daniel we're just friends. I ain't dating him."
"I'm messed up by that for real. Who does that? He's trying to watch you."
"And his ass will get an eyeful. I'm getting ready to do some laundry. I will talk to you later."
"Be careful Kelley. I will be by there later to pick up some clothes for Shemar."
"Okay, bye."
My phone rang.
"Hello."
"Hey Kelley, do you mind if I come down and wash with you?"
"That's fine."
"Okay, I will be down in a minute."
"Okay, bye."
My phone rang.
It was Daniel and I ignored him. Before I could load all my clothing in the machine, a noise startled me.
"Ain't that your baby daddy?"
"Where?"
"Staring in the window."
I looked up to my right and Daniel had his head pressed against the window with his hands hovered over his eyes. He banged on the window with his fist.
"What the hell is wrong with you?"
"Bring your ass out of there."
"What's wrong with him?"
Mark questioned Daniel.
"I don't know, but his ass needs to calm down."
"You better go see what he wants."
"As soon as I load my clothes."
I walked outside and Daniel started to yell, but I refuse to argue around my son. I ignored him and gave him a look that could kill. He got back in his car and pulled off. I took Shemar upstairs while Mark continued to do laundry.
My phone rang.

"Hello."

"Hey Kelley, since Mark is your man and sh*t, why don't you tell that nigga to take care of Shemar. Sh*t, I don't have to."

"You sound like a damn fool. Shemar is your son and what I do is none of your damn business. You are Shemar's father, and that has nothing to do with my personal life so mind your damn business."

"Tell that nigga to take him to school and pay child support."

"Daniel, I am not having this conversation with you. Good bye."

As I hung the phone up, Mark walked in.

"What's wrong with your baby daddy?"

"Don't come up here with no bullsh*t because I don't want to hear it. That nigga done lost his mind talking about, *why don't you be Shemar's daddy*. His ass is jealous. Oh well. He will get over it."

"He acts like y'all still f*cking."

"Bye Mark." I politely opened my front door.

*What the f*ck is wrong with them. Mark ole insecure, raggedy ass and Daniel has a lot of damn nerves. These niggas will not ruin my day.* I thought.

My phone rang.

"What Mark?"

"Hey Kelley, my fault; I was just wondering what was wrong with your baby daddy. So my fault."

"Thanks. I'm about to take Shemar to the park. I will talk to you later."

After I finished playing with Shemar at the park, I dropped him off at his God mother's house. I was ready to do what I did on Sunday evenings. The weather was perfect for my black halter top dress, and my black and white sandals with three-inch heels. My toes painted with white French tips and I was ready. I went to Genos, stepped a bit and had a couple of cocktails. On Sundays, I always went to Genos around six pm and many days I went home by midnight, but this particular day I left around nine p.m. On my way in the building, I saw a few of my guy friends standing in the back of the building. They were having cocktails, so I decided to join them. It was still early

and I didn't have to drive any more. At around ten pm, I walked down to Mark's house to surprise him.
"Marvin, will you walk down to Mark's house with me?"
"Who is Mark?"
"A friend of mine."
"I got you. Come on."
I knocked on Mark's door.
"Who is it?"
"Kelley."
Mark opened the door and Marvin stood at the top of the landing.
"Hey Mark."
"What's up? Mark wiped his eyes.
"I'm sorry, were you sleeping?"
"It's okay, come in."
"Come in Marvin. Mark, this is Marvin."
"What's up bro? It's good to meet you. Man Kels is like my sister man. You ain't gotta worry about nothing."
Marvin kissed me on the cheek and Mark looked at us with this strange look on his face.
"It's cool."
"Kels, you gon' be alright?"
"Yea, I'm cool."
"A'ight, it was nice to meet you Mark."
"You too."
Mark closed his door and immediately questioned me.
"What you bring him down here for?"
"I asked him to walk me down here because I didn't want to walk by myself."
"Where are you coming from?"
"I went to Genos for a while and on the way back, I saw them in the back so I had a cocktail with him and my other boys."
"You out there with a bunch of niggas with a short ass dress on drunk like a wh*re."
"Yep out there with my damn friends, dressed sexy as hell and feeling good now watch your damn mouth. Let me go home. I see you have an attitude. We're not a couple so why the hell are you worried about what I do?"

"You ain't gotta leave. You're right. Sit down for a minute."
"Sit down where."
I was drunk and did not want to sit on his air mattress. Mark didn't have any furniture other than a fish tank and a thirteen inch TV. His apartment was just like the first apartment I moved in.
"Stop touching me."
"What you come down here for?"
"I didn't come down here for this. I was about to leave, but you asked me to stay for a minute."
"Can I have a kiss?"
"No."
I dozed off and Mark's awoke me with his head between my legs.
"What the hell are you doing? Get off of me, Mark. Get your head from between my legs. What the f*ck?! I said get the f*ck off me. My screams echoed through his house. You stupid f*cking bastard! Motherf*cker! What the f*ck is wrong with you?"

I hastily walked out of his front door. *Crazy ass b*tch. This mother*cker better not even think about talking to me anymore.* I thought. When I dozed off, Mark smelled between my legs and then tried to lick my p*ssy. I didn't want him to touch me, and he knew I never had sex after drinking. I wasn't drunk, but not to the point I couldn't fight him off. I made it to my place and immediately passed out. I awoke the next morning, took a shower and noticed a bruise between my thighs. Mark bit me and left a black and purple bruise as wide as a Christmas tree ornament between my thighs. I rubbed the bruise and it was painful. *Lousy ass bastard, I oughta call the police on that mother*cker. He will never get that chance again.* I thought.

I dressed in shorts and a tank top and ran my errands. I made it home about four thirty and stopped to chat with a neighbor before going back inside. On my way in the building, Mark approached me.
"What the f*ck do you want?"

"I just came down here to talk to you."
"I ain't got sh*t to talk to you about."
"Don't bring no mother*cking niggas down to my crib again."
"Nigga, f*ck you. You ain't got to worry about that sh*t no more. Drunk or not, I remember what the f*ck you tried to do. You b*tch."
"What you call me?"
"B*tch you heard me. What the f*ck you gon' do? You tried to force yourself on me and you f*cking bit me. You lucky I don't call the police on your ass."
"You shouldn't have choked me with them big ass thighs."
"What the f*ck part of *stop* did you not understand? You abusive bastard."
"I'm not abusive."
"Nigga, you need some damn help. Somebody f*cked you up mentally. Maybe it was your mama or maybe some other chick, but you will not take that shit out on me. You need to see a damn therapist."
"I don't need to see a therapist. You need to see one."
"F*ck you Mark with your coward ass."
I turned away from Mark and walked into my building.
"Kelley wait, I'm sorry. When you brought that dude down there, I felt like you was disrespecting me."
"If you felt like I was disrespecting you, why the hell did you let us in? You assumed I was f*cking him. I don't know what type of women you've been dealing with, but I'm not them. Now leave me the f*ck alone. I'm going upstairs."
"Can we talk later?"
"For what? You won't get the chance to do that sh*t again."
"Kelley I'm sorry. It won't happen again."
"If you touch me again, I'm going to have someone beat your ass."
"I don't need to hear the threats."
"And I don't need your drama."
"Liquor makes me that way."

"You weren't even drunk so what's your excuse? It's one thing to react in violence while intoxicated, but to behave that was way sober; something is wrong with you. All the alcohol does is escalate the anger, but you weren't drunk. You have to see a therapist if you think I'm going to have anything else to do with you."
"I had a few drinks and what do I need to see a therapist for?"
"You have anger issues and you're abusive. I'm sure this isn't your first time hitting a woman."
"I didn't hit you. I bit you because you choked me with your big ass legs."
"Why did I choke you? Because you forced yourself on me. What makes you think you can behave aggressively towards any woman for any reason?"
"I don't want to talk about this sh*t. I'm not going to see any damn therapist and the only person need help is you. You're the one that's crazy. You're the reason I acted that way."
"You're not going to blame that sh*t on me. You must forget I know all the signs of an abusive person and you were abusive before you met me. You're going to hit the wrong woman one day and your ass will never raise your hand again."
I walked away from Mark and into my building. He showed all the signs of an abusive man from the beginning. I forgave him and allowed him back in. According to Dr. Phil, the anatomy of an abusive relationship is very simple. The cycle of violence has three stages and listed below, spells them out.

Tension Building Stage - When a victim suffers verbal abuse or minor physical violence, like slaps. At this stage, the victim may attempt to pacify the abuser. However, the victim's passivity may reinforce the abuser's violent tendencies.

Acute Battering Stage - At this stage, both perceived and real danger (of being killed or seriously injured) is maximal.http://www.statemaster.com/encyclopedia/Battered-woman-defence

- **Honeymoon Stage -** Dr. Phil says of the honeymoon stage, this is where, Oh, I'm sorry. I'm so sorry. I will never do this again. I hate that this happened. I'll make it up to you. I'm so sorry. I'm so sorry, but then the cycle starts over again. He notes that nearly half of abusers re-offend, most within the first six months. And then you've got what's called traumatic bonding, and it's because there's an imbalance of power, and there's an intermittent reinforcement schedule. You never know whether you're going to get hugged or hit. And so psychologically that's a very strong tendency to stay involved in that relationship.

http://www.drphil.com/articles/article/600

While reading, if you pay close attention to my relationship with Mark, you will see that Dr. Phil was correct about the stages of an abusive relationship.

June 2008
"Hello."
"Hey Kelley."
"Hey Mark, what's up?
"I'm on my way down there?"
"Okay."
"I made it." Mark came by to see me after work.
"How was work?"
"It was busy."
"Mark, are you going to go see a therapist?"
"Naw, liquor makes me that way. I had a few drinks and what do I need to see a therapist for. I'm not going to do it anymore."
"I don't trust you. You drink too much and I believe you will eventually swing and if you do, I will call the police on you."
"My other girlfriends didn't call the police on me when we fought."
"Mark please, that is pathetic. I wouldn't even tell anybody that sh*t. Those women tried to fight you or defend themselves, but I guarantee they lost. You're a man and only a coward hits a woman."
"I'm not going to allow a woman to say anything to me."

"What? You can't take words. Walk your ass away, but you don't hit a woman. I promise if you pull that sh*t with me again your ass is going to jail."
"So are we getting back together?"
"When you get a therapist."
"That's fine. I will try it. I'm not crazy."
"Therapy isn't for crazy people. It's to help you find any problems you might have. Did you see your mother get beat up by her boyfriend?"
"All the time. I saw him beating her up in the alley. Every time he was at our house, I would try to help and she would close the door on me. I remember when I was six or seven; she left me in the car while she looked for him."
"That's why you think it's normal for a man to hit a woman. You learned that from watching your mother."
"We really don't have a relationship. I love her, but we're not close. I didn't finish high school and neither did my sister, but my mother paid for my sister to take the G.E.D, and didn't pay for my test."
"Why don't you just go back to school?"
"I don't know man."
"Kennedy King has a program there. You should apply."
"Really. Maybe I will. I always wanted my High School diploma."
"Now you can go get it. Go after work or on Saturdays.
"I will call them this week."
"Good."
"Were you ever molested?"
"Naw, but this older boy, he was probably seventeen— tried to stick his d*ck in my butt when I was like seven or eight, but he didn't get it in."
"Who else knows about that?"
"Nobody."
"Did you ever tell your mother?"
"Nope, you're asking all these damn questions, have you ever been molested?"
"Yep, and I don't have a problem sharing, but this is about you and how you can overcome all this damn anger inside of you."
"You have something inside of you too."

"Nope, this ain't about me so don't try to flip the script. How old were you when you started masturbating?"

"My sister used to let me watch porn movies when I was eleven or twelve. That's when I started."

"You are an addict. You masturbate before sex, after sex, before work and when your daughter was over here. How many times do you masturbate a day?"

"Maybe three or four times."

"And you don't think something is wrong with that?"

"Not really, I just figured I was high natured."

"You might be, but think about it Mark. You started drinking at fifteen, masturbating at eleven, hitting women at eighteen, you started using cocaine as a teenager and you tried heroin. You date women who are underage. Don't you think there are some deep-rooted issues within you? No one just decides to use drugs and not think there's a problem. That alone is a hint that you didn't love yourself as a teen. You and I both know you weren't raised right, and there was a lack of love given to you from your parents. Your father was never around. How does all this sound to you? Why do you think you drink the way that you do. You are self-medicating. I can go on and on."

"So if I go to therapy, will you give me another chance?"

"Yea, but you have to go once a week."

"Okay. So how do I get a therapist?"

"Through your insurance with your job. Call the number on the back of your insurance card and they will get you started."

"Okay. I will."

"Now whoever the girl was you were seeing; you need to tell her to get lost. Just because I take a break away from you doesn't mean you go and get another girlfriend. Anybody would need time and space after dealing with you."

"How long did you wait after you and Daniel broke up?"

"It was two years before I met you. I dated people, but I refused to emotionally connect. Anyway, find a therapist, schedule an appointment, and I will take you to the first one, and then we can date again."

"As man and woman?"

"Yea Mark."

"Okay, I love you Kelley."
"You really shouldn't say that because when you love someone you don't cause them intentional pain. Everybody makes mistakes, but hitting someone is with the intent to hurt. Love doesn't hurt Mark. You have to love yourself first."
"I do love myself."
"If you loved yourself why do you abuse alcohol, drive drunk and hit women? Two of the three are grounds for prison. If you loved yourself, you wouldn't put yourself in harm's way, especially going to jail and losing your job."
"You drive drunk."
"You're right. Maybe we should quit, but you certainly need to slow down. You drink a pint of Seagram's Gin and a twenty-two ounce of Old English every day. What the hell?"
"One thing at a time, damn Kelley. I'm going home. You and Shemar can come down and have dinner with me if you like."
"That's fine. Just so you know, I don't ever want you around my son smelling like liquor and don't even think about behaving as his father. He has one."
"That's fine Kelley. Can I have some?"
"That's another story. Your sex is very abusive. You go to hard and fast. You don't know how to make love or be passionate. You need some lessons."
"So why don't you show me. How did you know I was seeing someone?"
"I have ears Mark and walking away in another room to talk silently on the phone is a sign. Anyway, you need to get rid of her."
"I was just using her for her link card."
"You're going to get enough of using and abusing women. I will see you in a minute."
Mark walked out my door and I shook my head from left to right.

August 2008
My unemployment was about to end, so I decided to look for a job and after three months of job searching, St. Francis Hospital hired me. I returned to work on August eleventh. I

was happy. I shared the news with family and friends, and of course Mark had nothing good to say.
"Hello."
"Hey Mark, I finally found a job."
"Good, because I'm sick of broke ass women."
"Ain't sh*t broke about me. The last time I checked, damn near the entire Summer I've been sponsoring your raggedy ass."
"Damn. I'm just playing."
"Play with someone who deserves to hear some sh*t like that. I've worked all my life and has been in healthcare now for sixteen years. How the hell do you think I'm off work? You're the one that just bought a car and didn't have a damn winter coat, cell phone or boots. All you know how to do is f*cking cook. You have lost your damn mind and if you sick of f*cking with broke women then maybe your broke ass need to check yourself."

I hung the phone up and Mark called back. I ignored the phone and he stopped calling. Three weeks passed and Shemar was on his way home. I was on Facebook and there was a knock on my door.
"Who is it?"
"Hey baby." I smiled, picked Shemar up and kissed his face.
"Hey Mommy."
"I miss you baby."
"I miss you too Mommy.
"Where is your dad?"
"He left already."
"Okay, did you have fun with your dad?"
"Yep."
"Keep your coat on. We're going to the store."
"Can I have a toy?"
"You sure can. Come on baby."

*His ass is still mad about Mark. I really don't know what for. I'm not f*cking him. He needs to get over it.* I thought. I kept all the nonsense away from my son. Not once did I ever argue around my son with Mark or his daddy for that matter. I had no problem opening my front door and telling either of them to leave if they ever became loud or disrespectful around my son. If anyone would be loud and cuss around my son it would be me.

My phone rang.
"Hello."
"What's up Kelley? I just called to apologize for the incident a few weeks ago. That was wrong and you're right, your personal life is none of my business."
"Thank you, I mind my business and stay out of yours."
"I know and I appreciate that. So, I'm sorry and it won't happen again."
"Good."
"How was Shemar's party?"
"It turned out great. Shemar had so much fun. You should have been there."
"Yea, I know, my fault man. Do you mind if I stop by and get him later?"
"Yea, that's cool. I have to work anyway."
"That's right. You're working night-shift now."
"Yep, back in business."
"Okay, I will call you when I'm on my way."
"Okay, bye."

The entire summer was mental and physical stress, call offs, hospital visits, and running back and forth to Ms. Harris's house to pick Shemar up. Shemar constantly called me and wanted me to come get him. For whatever reason, he wanted out of that house when his father wasn't home. I found out later, but that's another book.

The stress from Daniel and Mark caused my body to break down. All the knowledge I had about abuse, yet I was in my first physically abusive relationship. Although the physical abuse didn't happen often, it happened. I hated myself for having anything to do with Mark. He was nothing but a big cock and a pretty face. Mark was a mentally unstable and abusive man and I knew it, but who was I to criticize him. I was f*cking him. The sight of Mark made me want to cringe and many days, I wanted to stab him seventy-two times in the chest. But I didn't. I continued to accept the unnecessary drama and games he played.

December 2008
I sat down, logged on Face Book and posted indirect negative comments about Mark. My mind became overcrowded with thoughts of my past life. I thought I was having a panic attack. *Why am I having these thoughts? Maybe it's the book I'm supposed to write.* I thought. Josh suggested I write a book back in April after I completed a speech for a class of graduates, but I wasn't interested. In the past, I thought about writing a book, but never put it into action. I called Josh and asked for his help. After a month of working with him, I was on my way to writing and publishing my first book. I really didn't know what to expect and had no idea of what was to come. Day in and day out I typed; night after night; at work, at home, and even at the library. I committed myself to finishing my book.

Mark was very jealous and always complained about my writing when he came to visit. He was not supportive at all and I didn't care. I was never one to start something and not finish. My everyday became about my book and Shemar; nothing else mattered. I wrote religiously for the next four months and was very proud of myself. Most of my co-workers supported me and looked forward to reading my story. I had no idea my first book would ultimately change my life in more ways than I could imagine.

January 2009

My relationship with Mark was on and off from the beginning. I cared about him, but I really didn't want him and didn't want anyone else to have him. How lame was that? He was an abusive, alcoholic, cheating, drug addict whom I suspected him of being on the down-low. I broke up with Mark at least four times in this past year. He reminded me of Chrissy's ex-boyfriend, Kenneth and Nicki's ex-boyfriend, Veto. I hated men who hit women. I had no respect for them. All it took was for Mark to say the wrong word to me and he would've been every stupid, dumb b*tch in the book. I had no problem cussing him out in the worst way.

Mark spent a night at my house and left his phone on my night stand.

My phone rang.
"Hello."
"Kelley, I left my phone at your house."
"I know, it will be here when you get off."
"Okay, I have to get back to work."
Mark's phone rang.
"Hello."
"May I speak to Mark?"
"Who's calling?"
"This is his friend Evelyn."
"He's in the bathroom. I will tell him you called."
"Okay."

I hung the phone up and looked at the caller I.D. The caller ID said, *Real Estate*. Evelyn was Mark's first girlfriend and they reconnected around the same time I met him, so he said, but Mark told me he wasn't talking to her anymore, and she had a man. A few seconds later a text message came through on Mark's phone.

Hey Mark. I just called your phone and your girl answered it.
I text back
This is Kelley, Mark's woman. Why are you calling and texting him?

I waited for a response and nothing, so I deleted the messages. I was furious because Mark told me he wasn't talking to her any more. I looked at the phone again and waited patiently for him to come to my house.
"Hey Mark, how was your day?"
"It was fine."
Mark immediately grabbed his phone off my nightstand.
"You had a phone call from some Real Estate company."
"Cool, I've been looking at houses."
"Really, call them back. Maybe they found something."
"I will wait until I get home."
"Mark you must think I'm stupid. I answered your phone and it was Evelyn. I thought you said you weren't talking to her anymore."
"Why the f*ck did you answer my phone?"
"Why the f*ck is it a problem if you're not cheating? Get the f*ck out of my house. I don't have time for any lying, abusive, dog ass nigga. You said you weren't talking to her anymore, and your ass lied so you're still f*cking her."
"Kelley, Kelley, please I'm sorry. Please don't leave me."
Mark dropped to his knees and grabbed my legs.
"Get up Mark. You can go be with the b*tch with your lying ass."
"Kelley, I promise I will tell her to stop calling me."
"Mark, I don't want this sh*t in my life. You can do whatever you want."
"Kelley, please don't leave me."
Mark's eyes' filled with tears.
"You can go some damn where with those crocodile ass tears. I'm not falling for that sh*t. Get the f*ck out my house."
"Watch your f*cking mouth."
"Or what? You're gonna hit me. Then what? You are still getting the f*ck out my house."
I walked to my front door, opened it and waited for Mark to leave. He stood there in my bedroom doorway looking stupid.
"Kelley, will you please close the door?"
"Bye Mark."
"This sh*t is your fault. You're always leaving me."

"Get the f*ck out my house before I call the police and have your ass arrested for trespassing."
"F*ck you."
"F*ck you, stupid bastard."

I slammed the door. Mark left and I was furious. I called his phone many times and called him every name known to humanity. A few weeks passed before I talked to him again. I refuse to harbor any more pain and anger in my heart so I forgave him again.

Mark invited me out and we went to play spades and bid whiz at one of his friend's houses. I could see that drunken look in Mark's eyes. When he stood, he staggered. I asked for his keys so I could drive. Mark refused.

"You are f*cking drunk and you have no business driving."
"I got this so you can shut the f*ck up."
"This is just damn ridiculous."

I sat quietly so Mark could focus on the road. The roads were very slippery and he drove wo lanes. I freaked out on the inside. By the time we got closer to home, Mark drove faster.
"You really need to slow down, especially going to the back of the building."
"I got this."

Mark increased his speed to about forty-five miles per hour on Cochran Street and headed toward the back of our building. I could see the railroad tracks facing us. I was sure he would drive directly on the tracks. Right before we hit the tracks, Mark turned and swerved directly into a snow bank preventing us from flipping over and on the tracks. His rear, passenger side tire popped off. He parked, and I politely exited his car and walked down the street to my place.

*This nigga could have killed me. I am out of my f*cking mind to even be friends with him. Lord, I need some help.* I thought.
"Where are you going?"

"I'm going away from your crazy drunk ass."

April 2009
"It's eleven o'clock in the morning and you're already drunk. Damn. How much did you have?"
"I didn't have much."
"Why is your speech slurred and why are staggering?"
"I'm good and I'm about to go fishing. I just came over to get the cooler."
"For more drinks I suppose."
"Yea, that's what I do when I fish."
"Just go to the bank and get the money you owe me."
"You can follow me to the bank."
"That's fine."
Driving west on one hundred and twenty-seventh street, I noticed Mark swerved between two lanes. I reached for my cell phone so I could call the police. *I ought to have this nigga arrested. This mother*cker is drunk as hell. F*ck him. I just want my damn money.* I thought. I parked my car in the Ultra Foods parking lot and waited for him to bring my money.
"Here."
"Thank you."
I pulled off.
Later in the week, I invited Mark and his son out with my niece and me. We had a pretty good time until we were on our way home. Mark's son cried and talked about how Mark wasn't there for as a child. We knew it was the liquor talking, but it was the truth. Mark didn't like what he heard so things got really ugly. I tried to calm him down, but it didn't work. We pulled up in the front of my building and Mark snapped. He was very loud and I know the neighbors heard him. Before I knew it, he got out of his car and walked around to my side.
"Get the hell away from me. Let my damn arm go Mark. What the hell is wrong with you? Stop!"

He pulled my arm and tried to pull me out of his car. I could hear my niece screaming at him, and his son telling him to let me go, but he refused. Losing my grip on the steering wheel, Mark pulled me out of his car and threw me to the ground. He then walked hastily back to the driver's side and got in his car. I got up and slammed my shoe against his window and tried to break it. I called the police and described Mark to them. I gave the police his license plate number, but before they got there, Mark pulled off and hid somewhere. His son did not want to go home with him because he was afraid of Mark. I allowed his son to spend a night at my place. The police came by my house to talk, and make sure
Mark wasn't there. The next morning Mark came down to get his son and we argued. He apologized again and like a fool I accepted. I was pissed at him and wanted someone to beat his ass. I talked to a few of the guys in the neighborhood and asked them to beat Mark's ass. These were the older teenagers I fed on many occasions, holidays or just any day. They took a liking to me and considered me a big sister. A couple of days later, they were only a few feet away from Mark and I couldn't go through with it.

June 2009
"Mark, are you still going to make the spaghetti for me?"
"Yea, I got you."
"I cooked all the other food, so after the spaghetti, we can chill and wait for everybody to get here."
"Okay, I'm going to cook it now."
"Thanks."
I wanted to have a party, because many of the people I hadn't seen were coming. I threw a party at least once a month. On the menu was jerk chicken, salad, spaghetti, tacos, chips and dip. I had one fifth of Ciroc, one fifth of Courvoisier and several cases of Millers Genuine Draft, and Budweiser. Anyone who came to my party was aware of me starting the party with liquor, but everybody had to "BYOB," bring your own bottle. Everything was going great. People were playing spades, throwing darts, dancing, sitting, eating, laughing and talking.

"Hey Tank, I see you made it."
"Girl you are my big sister. I wasn't going to miss this. I've been hearing about your parties since you moved over here."
"Are you hungry?"
"Yea, I'm not staying long. I just came to throw one back with you and get some food."
"That's cool, come on in. Go ahead and help yourself to a plate and I will be in there in a second."
"Why is this nigga here?"
Mark sat on my bed with that angry drunken look.
"Ain't that the same nigga you said was going to kick my ass."
"Yep, so what, did he touch you?"
"You need to tell him to leave."
"Why would I do that, and I invited him?"
"You invited that nigga?"
"This is my party and my apartment. I can do as I feel."
"Did you really just punch a hole in the wall? I don't have time for this sh*t. There are too many people here. You can either chill the f*ck out and fix that sh*t tomorrow or leave now. It's up to you, but you're not going to ruin my party."
"Man f*ck this sh*t, I want that nigga out."
"I'm going back to the front to entertain my guest. You can sit back here angry if you want."
I walked out of my bedroom and to the living, and continued to host my party. I didn't care about the wall, and I was not going to let Mark ruin my party. I guess he wasn't happy with my decision.
"Kelley!"
"What Mark?"
"So I see the nigga just left. Why didn't you put his ass out when I told you to?"
"Mark you need to let this sh*t go before I put you out."
"I don't give a f*ck."
"Ok, then leave."
"I'm not going any damn where."
"Yes, you are."

I walked to the front and grabbed a few of my friends and family members. We walked back to my bedroom and stood there.

"Bye Mark."

Mark looked at everybody in complete silence. He had no win and his time was up. I opened the door, stood there and waited for him to leave. Mark walked out with this evil look on his face as if he wanted to swing.

"Mark, get the f*ck on gone and don't even think about hitting her or you will get f*cked up. Damenia stood strong with her fist balled. Mark left and we continued to party until about four o'clock in the morning. At about nine o'clock in the morning I awoke to the sounds of banging on my front door, and of course it was Mark. My head pounded from too many shots of Tequila.

"What's up Mark?"

"I came to fix the wall. I already asked the maintenance man for some spackle."

"That's fine. Go ahead and fix it."

"You ain't got nothing else to say?"

"Nope, I'm not dealing with you this morning."

"I'm sorry about the wall."

"You're always sorry. I told you I didn't care about the wall as long as you fixed it. But you wanna get mad and try to control sh*t. You haven't caught on yet. You will never control me, so stop trying. You really need to see a therapist. I'm going back to bed. My head hurts and your apologies are wasted air."

"Yea a'ight Kelley, I will fix the wall and leave. Can I call you later?"

"I will call you when I wake up."

I didn't call Mark for a few days, but when I did, he was in school and made an appointment for therapy. I was proud of him for making those decisions. But the biggest questions were, would he finish school, and would he be honest with the therapist about the problems he shared with me. Time passed and Mark did well in school and saw his therapist once a week.

August 2009

"Kelley, can I borrow four hundred dollars?"

"Until when, and how are you going to pay me back? Aren't you having financial problems?"

"You know I just received a promotion and a bonus came with it. I should have it in a month or so."

"Okay, that's cool. I want all my money back Mark."

I didn't have a problem loaning Mark money. As friends, we did well looking out for each other. It was easier to be cool with him without sex.

"How is your new job?"

"Everything is great, but my hours will change soon, so I might have to quit school."

"Why? Can't you ask them to accommodate you for your education?"

"They're not going to do that. Besides, I'm making more money so that's good enough for me."

"I thought you wanted your G.E.D."

"I did, but not having it hasn't stopped anything."

"I would hate to see you lose your job and have to look for another one. Companies do not want to hire anyone without a G.E.D or high school diploma. But that's your choice."

"I'm good and my boss is cool as hell."

"That's good Mark."

"How is therapy?"

"I figured a few things out so I will be okay."

"Don't give up on therapy."

"I'm good Kelley."

Mark and his new boss had a tight relationship. I thought it was quite strange since my knowledge of management made me question their relationship. I understood bosses were not to have a personal relationship with employees. That entire relationship just didn't sit well with me.

October 2009 - Halloween

Mark and I planned on taking Shemar trick or treating later that night. I called off work because of all the stress and I lost my desire to work. A part of me wanted things to work between Mark and me. While Mark cooked dinner for his mother, I went back to my place to get my outfit together. I came back and we had a few cocktails.

"Kelley, don't rush me?"
"What are you talking about?"
"You keep asking me what time will I be ready."
"I only asked you twice and you never answered the first time."
"I'm making dinner for my mother, so don't rush me."
"I don't know where you're going with this, but I'm not rushing you. You're letting that liquor get to you and now you're ready to start some sh*t. I'm going to Mr. Submarine and get Shemar a sandwich."
"I want one too, so I'll go with you."

I dropped Mark off at his house and went home. We got into a huge argument on the telephone and I went back down to his house to get a few items I left down there. I wanted to cuss him out. I would've gone to work if I knew he was going to act like an ass.

"When are you going to give me my four hundred dollars?"
"I'm not giving you sh*t."
"Yes the f*ck you are."

I slapped his sandwich off the table and walked towards the kitchen. Moments later I felt a hard blow to the back of my head and I screamed. I grabbed a red plate out of Mark's reddish dish rack and I threw it at him. It hit the fish tank. I then grabbed a fork and he charged towards me and pushed me to the ground. My hand was bleeding. Five feet from me was his tan house phone attached to the wall, and I grabbed it. I dialed nine one one and Mark tried to snatch the phone from my hand, but the dispatcher located the address.

"B*tch you're going to jail now."
"I'm not going anywhere?"

Mark sat on his red loveseat as I opened his door, and waited for the police to arrive.

"Did someone call the police?"

"Yes, I did. I want him arrested for hitting me."
"Who are you and whose place is this?"
"My name is Kelley and he is my boyfriend, and he just hit me in the back of my head."
"No, I didn't. I didn't touch her lying ass. This is my apartment officer. She came down here starting sh*t and she knocked my food out of my hand. It's all over the walls."
"Yes, I did knock his sandwich off the table. But that did not give him a right to hit me."
"Where did he hit you?"
"In the back of my head."
"Did he hit you with an open hand or fist?"
"Open hand."
"Turn around ma'am, and let me take a look. Why is your hand bleeding?"
"After he hit me he shoved me on the floor and I cut my hand on this glass."
"How did this plate get broken?"
"She started breaking my stuff."
"Sir, be quiet."
"I threw a plate at him after he hit me and one fell to the ground."
"Turn around; I don't see any bruises."
"What happened sir?"
"She came down here and started an argument and she left her baby at home by himself."
"He's lying officer, and he's trying to get out of hitting me."
"Where is your son?"
"He's with his grandmother."
"I don't see any evidence of bruises ma'am. Get your stuff and go home. If we get another call from this address, sir, you're going to jail. Ma'am, do not come back down here."
"So he hits me, lies about it and you believe him. I have blood all over my hand and you don't believe me."
"Ma'am, you're in his place and I don't see any bruises."
"What the hell do you call this bleeding from my hand?"
"I didn't hit her officer."

Mark sat there in his red loveseat with his arm resting on the armrest and his legs wide apart with this deceitful look on his face.
"You know what, f*ck it. You will get yours."

I left Mark's place and walked to his mother's. I told her what happened and his sister Tasha told me, he beat every woman he's been involved with over the last twenty years. She also told me he choked his daughter's mother, knocked her across a room, blacked her eye, slapped her, and beat all his past girlfriends. He was a very angry and abusive man with a history of drug use. Even after he bit me, drug me out of his car, pushed me to the ground, hit me in the back of my head, and this information, I still allowed Mark back in my life. Months passed before I even considered having anything else to do with Mark. Therapy didn't help him and in January of 2010, I learned something else about Mark and up to this current day, I believe to be true.

I cried for many days because I knew the relationship with Mark was unhealthy and dangerous. I also missed him. I thought I could help him. I thought if he understood his problems, he would get the help he needed. Instead, he blamed me for all his violent behavior and told me I was crazy. I was even willing to go to therapy with him to find out if I was provoking him. That thought left my mind immediately. I was one hundred percent sure Mark was unstable, and abusive long before he met me. The rest of the fall and half of the winter passed before I became friends with him again. Mark tried to convince me he would never hit me again, and seven months passed before he stepped out of line again. That day was the straw that broke the camel's back. I hated myself for allowing this poor treatment. I was no longer a child and in full control. I decided to continue to see Mark and for that I hold myself accountable for everything that happened. I don't blame myself for his behavior, but I knew enough from the beginning to run and run fast.

The stress was so overwhelming, the doctors at Metro South admitted me twice during the time we dated. I developed chest pain, dizziness, shortness of breath and my right arm went numb sometimes. I learned in the hospital, I suffered from panic attacks. I never told anyone because of the shame. The shame and embarrassment came from me allowing someone to abuse me physically, yet I knew so much about abuse. I didn't need his money, he didn't control me, and I wasn't afraid of him. The truth of the matter was, I wanted Mark to love me. I still desperately wanted a man to love me. I was very familiar with abuse, but the physical abuse was not something I was willing to sit by and take. There was something inside me that wanted Mark's head cut off.

November 2009
I was at work and it was about one o'clock in the morning when my phone rang.
"Hello."
"Hey Kelley."
"What's up Mark?"
"Do you mind if I stop by your job for a moment? I need to talk to you about a few things."
"What's wrong with you?"
"Aint nothing wrong with me."
"You sound like you're pissed off."
"Damn, can I just come up there?"
"That's fine, but don't bring the damn attitude."
Mark and I weren't dating, but we talked occasionally. I went downstairs to walk him pass security, and we made it back to the lab.
"What did you need to come up here for?"
"I went out with my boss Ben and some of the guys from work and me and Ben were the last two to leave. While we cleaned the snow off of our cars, he had the nerve to tell me *there ain't nothing wrong with two men being together and then asked me if he could have a kiss.* Then he asked me *what's inside of my pants and said everybody wants some of that.*"

Ben was Mark's boss and was fat, brown-skinned and walked with a switch. The way he stared at Mark would have easily made any woman feel uneasy about him being around.

"Are you serious? Mark I told you that dude was gay and you defended him. You told me *I was jealous you had a six figure friend*. Now that nigga has shown you his true colors. I knew something wasn't right when he gave you that two thousand dollar bonus. So why did you need to come up here? Isn't he married? Why don't you tell his wife or report him? Didn't you tell me he was making passes at you during work hours? This sh*t is crazy."
"I let him stay at my place because he got so drunk he couldn't drive back to Indiana. I didn't want to stay there with him. He's married, but I don't want to tell his wife. If I report him, I might lose my job."
"So he's at your place now? So what are you going to do?"
"If you don't mind, I'd like to sit here for another hour or two. He said he just needed to lie down for an hour or so."
"How did he get in your house?"
"I let him in and left."
"That just doesn't even sound right. He probably wants to f*ck you."
"How do you know he don't want me to f*ck him?"
"You're a man and that just doesn't even sound right coming out of your damn mouth. Let me finish my work."
I continued to do my work and the look on Mark's face was very uncomfortable and my suspicions were overwhelming. *Why the hell would anyone hang out with their boss if he's been sexually harassing him? Why would he accept money from him? Why is he in his apartment now? This nigga is probably gay.* I thought. That whole situation wasn't right. Eventually Mark left and the next day he called to tell me his boss apologized, and said it wouldn't happen again.

January 2010
Mark had a New Year's gathering at his house and invited me, Nicki, Chrissy, Damenia, my niece Tee and his boss Ben. The

moment everybody saw Ben, gay immediately surfaced into their heads.

"Girl this nigga got a five-pound bag of sugar in his ass."
Tee laughed.
"That's Mark's boss."
"Why is he hanging with Mark?"
Chrissy questioned Ben.
"Why are they toasting a glass of champagne together? What the f*ck? Kelley is he gay?"
Damenia shook her head from left to right.
"The hell if I know, I'm not dating his ass so he could be whatever he wants."

Ben and Mark eventually joined us in the living room and sat right next to each other. Mark didn't appear uncomfortable. He smiled and enjoyed his red wine with Ben. We all made small talk, but the setting was too awkward. We left and went down to my place.

"Girl I would hate to think that Mark's fine ass is gay. Why is his boss hanging with him?" Chrissy asked the same questions I asked.

"From what Mark told me, I know his boss is gay. Mark said he's from Philadelphia and doesn't know anyone up here so he's looking for some friends."

"His grown ass can find some friends on his own. That nigga wants to suck Mark's d*ck." Damenia knew Ben was gay.

Everybody laughed. After seeing Mark so comfortable with his gay boss, I was really turned off by him. We never got back together. We just remained cool and Mark became a convenience to me. He saw other women and on occasion, I dated other men. That hit in the back of the head was too much for me. I knew if I stayed it would get worse. I decided to stay clear of Mark and be cool with him. From time to time we helped each other out or had a cocktail together. He finally paid my four hundred dollars back, and I never loaned him anything more than twenty dollars after that.

February 2010

I wasn't feeling Mark these days and wanted to have sex with someone else. I went to Genos on a Saturday night and there was a young woman who I found attractive. I never said anything to her before, but this day, I found the courage. She was very interested and wanted to come home with me. I told her if she was serious she can call me the next day. She did. This has been what my body desired since day one; one on one with a woman and no man. She made it to my house around two o'clock the next day, and after a couple of hours she left.

Later that day, I sat down at my computer and began to write in my book. While writing in the chapter "The Ring Leader," I shared my introduction to being sexual with girls. By the time I was in the chapter "Desperately Seeking Love," I immediately compared both chapters and at that time, I realized where the lust came from. I pushed away from my black computer desk and dropped to my knees.

"O God. Please help me. I do not want this. I did not ask for this. God please take this lust for women away from me. I am not gay, lesbian or bisexual. Please remove this lust from me. Please God. I am begging."

I cried. My nostrils filled with mucus and tears flowed down my cheeks. Tear after tear, I begged the Lord to heal me; to remove the lust that was a direct product of the incest and sexual coercions I experienced as a child. I cried and cried. I prayed as I sat on my knees thinking about all the years I walked around confused about my sexual preference; lusting for women and acting on those feelings. I wanted no parts of it. I wanted no parts of anything from my past life a part of my present. Two weeks later, I passed an unexpected test. I went out to Tommy's in Blue Island to watch the basketball game and to my surprise there were lesbian women present. I looked, and then looked away. I ate my buffalo wings and continued to watch the game. I looked around again and the club crowded with lesbian women. I decided to leave.

My desire for women was gone. For so long, I never realized being sexually introduced to girls at such a young age was the reason as a teen, and an adult, I thought I was bisexual. I claimed bisexuality, partied in the lesbian, gay, transgender, community and slept with many women. I was **never** bisexual. I lived confused about my sexuality and preference because of the sexual introduction to girls and boys as a child. Being molested by the same sex does not make you gay. It makes you a victim of a vicious sex crime. It confuses you, but it doesn't make you gay. Make the connection.

March 2010
"Hello."
"Hey Mark. Are you still going to help me put up my new kitchen set?"
"Yea, give me a minute. I'm cooking breakfast."
"Oh cool, I'm coming down there."
"For what?"
"To get a plate."
I walked down to Mark's apartment and he made eggs, bacon, hash browns, toast and grits. He also had a bottle of red wine.
"Who did you make breakfast for?"
"Ben is about to stop by and bring some paperwork I need for the job."
"Oh."
Moments later there was a knock at the door. I opened the door.
"Hi Kelley."
"How are you Ben?"
"I'm great."
"Hey Mark." Ben smiled.
"What's going on boss?" Mark smiled.
Ben took his shoes off with complete comfort and the way he sat down was unbelievable. He opened his legs and proceeded to a squat position over the couch. He then poked his ass in the air before landing it on the couch. I was blown the hell away.
"Mark y'all have fun." I walked out of his door.

*What the f*ck? This nigga just sat down like a straight up b*tch. Mark faggot ass is down there making him breakfast. I hate to assume anything, but that nigga is gay as all outdoors.* I thought as I walked to my building.

That was not the worse part of it. By the middle of spring 2010, nothing could make me think Mark wasn't a down low brother. I knew at some point in his life he received a d*ck in his ass.

April 2010
Mark and I were in the middle of sex, and he wanted me to do something I never thought any man would ask of a woman. I was very uncomfortable, but he insisted.
"Kelley a doctor told me if a man is getting his d*ck sucked and a woman sticks her finger in his ass, he would get the best orgasm."
"I've heard that before. Is that what you want to try?"
"I do, but I don't. I'm scared." Mark chuckled and shook his body.
"Have you ever done this before?"
"No."
"So what do you want me to do?"
"While you're giving me head, I will tell you what to do."
Mark laid on his back and raised his legs up in the air. I looked at him confused as he was too comfortable in this position. This position was known to women and my mind immediately wandered.
"Put your finger in, wait, put some grease on your finger."
I was in total shock. I got out of the bed and grabbed the Vaseline. I greased my middle finger and Mark threw his legs in the air again.
"Okay. I'm ready.

I moved my finger around his anal area because this was not something I had ever done in my life, and I had done some things. His next behavior shocked me. I was very uncomfortable and thought I would hurt him like he hurt me before this day.

Mark and I were going to attempt anal sex. One day I was on my stomach and he knew he was way too large. I told him to go slowly and without notice he shoved his large d*ck in my ass. I lost my breath and was frozen. My facial expression wreaked pain and I couldn't breathe. I started to cry, and Mark removed his d*ck out of my ass. I told him to leave my house and never tried it again. I felt violated because he never warned me. I believe he wanted to hurt me and more than often, he did.

"Put it in."
"Give me a minute. This is new to me."
"Put it in!" Mark aggressively shoved my finger in his ass.
"Now move it back and forth."
Before I realized it, I was finger f*cking Mark in his ass.
"Okay, that's enough. It wasn't what people say, but it wasn't bad.

That day was enough for me to never assume again. I knew Mark was a bisexual, down low brother. I rolled over, got out the bed, went in the bathroom and washed my hands. *This nigga was too comfortable with the way he spread his legs. He shoved my finger in his ass. What man does that? I need to have myself checked for Aids. Got damn.* I thought.

"Kelley, I'm going to the crib."
"Ok."
Mark left and I couldn't stop myself from calling him and questioning his sexuality. We were far from boyfriend and girlfriend, but from time to time we had sex.
"What's up Kelley?"
"I have a question? Are you sure you haven't done that before? You were too comfortable with the way you lifted, and spread your legs, and then to shove my finger in your ass. I know you told me when you were younger an older male teen tried to molest you."
"Yea, but he didn't get it in."
"Okay, so why were you so comfortable?"

"I wasn't comfortable. I knew I shouldn't have done sh*t with you. Ain't nobody said sh*t about you sucking p*ssy. When you were licking my ass, you acted like it was a p*ssy."
"Why are you getting so mad and defensive?"
"I'm not getting defensive. I don't appreciate you questioning me and I'm not talking about this sh*t."
Mark hung the phone up and his defense, yelling and attacks on me were more confirmation.

May 2010

Mark invited me on a trip to the Bahamas with him and I was skeptical about going with him. He paid for the trip and I was to pay for the flight to Florida. I wasn't interested in him anymore and Lord knows I didn't want him touching me sexually again. I couldn't remove the thoughts of him letting me finger f*ck him.

"Hello."
"Hey Kelley, I'm glad you decided to take the trip with me. I didn't want to go by myself."
"It's cool, as long as you know we're going as friends."
"I'm cool with that. I just want to fly and go on a cruise. I'm going to stop by when I get off work."
"That's fine.
Mark made it to my place and it didn't end well.
"Who is it?"
"Mark."
"Hey Kelley."
"Hey, I'm on the phone."
"Carla you need to lock his ass up if he hit you. Don't let him get away with that."
"Would you get off the phone?"
"Hold on Carla."
"I didn't ask you to come down here. Now you could either wait or leave."
"Carla, I'm back. Call the police and call me back."
"Why are you all up in their business?"
"If that nigga hits her, he needs to go to jail."
"Whatever Kelley, did you get the tickets?"

"Yep, here is the confirmation receipt. I also added insurance."
"Good, why did you tell Carla to lock my boy up?"
"Because he jumped on her and that's what she needs to do."
"Kelley you need to mind your damn business."
"Why don't you leave my damn house? Your ass is mad because I called the police on your ass. I don't give a f*ck about a b*tch ass nigga who hits a woman. All of them are cowards and trash."
Mark picked up his cup of juice and threw it on me.
"That was your last f*cking time. I hope to see the next woman you hit, knock your damn brain out. Get out my house."

I walked toward my front door, opened it, tore the tickets up, and slammed the door on Mark's heel as he walked out. That was the straw that broke the camel's back. Mark and I ended. Over the summer, Mark and I remained in contact through talking and helping each other if needed. I actually missed his barbeques, fishing trips, and him cooking breakfast or dinner for me. I did not miss the abuse, his insecurities or his controlling ways. The fact that he lived in the same complex and walking distance from me, made it hard to stay away, and the fact that I still cared about him. But Mark knew it was over. Mark left for his trip to the Bahamas and each day he was gone he called to tell me, he missed me. I needed that break away from him. I needed to clear my head and gain enough strength to stay as far away from him as possible. For some sick reason, I didn't stay far away. I realized I was no better than Mark.

I accepted the abuse and didn't have to. I accepted the name calling, the lies, the betrayal, the stress and the physical abuse. My self-worth wasn't where I thought it was. I walked in the darkness when I thought I walked in the light. Before I move forward, I'd like to share a few reasons why women end up in domestic violence, or bad relationships, and why they stay. Please understand, no woman wants a man to hit or disrespect her. This list does not exclude men.

Kelley Porter

Why do women end up in abusive or bad relationships?
Lack of knowledge of domestic violence.
They do not know or recognize red flags (warning signs)
Women ignore the red flags
A history of child abuse from parents or siblings
Desperate to have a man and accept anything
Afraid and lack the confidence to be alone
Some women only know abuse and was never taught love
They were fatherless daughters
Their fathers physically abused them
Lack of self-love and self-worth
Some believe they can change an abusive man
Some do not understand love and has never seen a healthy relationship
Some are conditioned to toxic or abusive relationships

Why do women stay?
According to McHenry County Turning Point, listed below are some of the behaviors that keep a woman from leaving an abuser.

Fear
Fear of physical harm
Fear of threats
Fear of harassment
Fear of making abuser angrier
Fear of living alone or being alone
Fear of losing children
Fear of losing the house, car
Fear others will blame you
Fear of the unknown
Fear of financial problems without him
Fear of a change in standard of living
Fear of deportation
Fear no one believes you
Fear of the court system

Love
Still loves the abuser

Commitment to the relationship
Sex, affection, and kindness during non-violent times
Companionship
History together
Hope it's going to improve
Hope he'll change

Emotional
Low self-esteem
Being emotionally exhausted
Loneliness
Guilt
Self-blame for the abuse
Feeling like a failure
Feeling defective
Feeling unwanted by others

Change
Not wanting a divorce
Not wanting to be a single parent
Not wanting to look for someone else
Not wanting to leave pets
Not wanting to grieve
Not wanting to start over
Not wanting to change life style
Not wanting to lose his family
Not wanting to be excluded from social functions

Abuser
Uses mind games
Uses crying
Uses threats of suicide
Uses his power and his family's power
Uses his Mr. Nice Guy image
Uses promises
Uses apologies

Kelley Porter

Children
Pressure from children who want their dad
Believes it is best for children
Custody issues
Need childcare

Support
Nowhere to go
Unaware help is available
No support system
Isolated from support

Needs
Need insurance
Need financial support
Have health/disability issues

More
Not identifying abuse
Normalize abusive behaviors
Abusive cycle is familiar
Others accept violence as okay
Pressure from others
Preserve abusers reputation
Religious beliefs
Social status
Security
Having hopes and dreams
Same sex partners
Knowing it's okay to leave

Why did I stay?
Low self-esteem
Lack of self-worth
Lack of self-love
I thought I could change him
I was desperate for a man
I wanted to be loved by a man

http://www.mchenrycountyturningpoint.org/powerandcontrol.html

December 2010
Mark dated a woman 12 years younger than him named Keke. Although I wanted Mark gone, I was still jealous and angry. I was jealous and angry because, on occasion, I slept with him. I didn't want anyone having him, and I felt defeated. Mark made sure I knew of his new girlfriend. He wanted to hurt me, and he did. We talked on the phone, and he mentioned his new girlfriend to me. It bothered me, but I knew I had to let Mark go. Eventually, I found peace, and although Mark abused me, I was able to forgive him and ask for forgiveness. I apologized and asked for forgiveness because I said and did some very mean things to him. Most of what I told him was in self-defense, and because I couldn't control my anger. I didn't have to stoop to his level and hit him below the belt. I could have only walked away because I knew better. I knew from the beginning Mark was abusive, and I had no business dating a man who had a woman, let alone to think he would treat me better than how he treated his daughter's mother. I was wrong from the beginning. Did I deserve the abuse? Not. Am I accountable? Yes. Let's set aside; he had a woman, the first time he tried to pull me out of his car was the moment I should have run. But I didn't, and for that, I must hold myself accountable.

January 2011
"Hello."
"Hey Mark."
"Do you have a can of tomato paste?"
"Kelley, I have Keke over and I can't bring anything over there."
"You didn't have to answer the phone if you have company."
"Anyway, what do you want?"
"I just told you, but I'm not trying to cause any problems."
"Did you want to see me?" Mark handed KeKe the phone.

"Not really. Why would I want to see you? I'm not even interested in talking to you. But I will say this; you have no idea who you are dating. Mark is very abusive and if you think he's going to treat you any different, I feel sorry for you."
"I know Mark better than you and maybe you're the reason he hit you. He told me about the situation in the kitchen. Maybe you could have done things differently."
"Sweetheart, you're young and I don't know what he told you, but you will find out soon enough."
"My age doesn't mean anything and Mark is a good man. He just needs a good woman."

"I guess he told you I was a horrible woman. Did you know he told me the same thing about his daughter's mother before he put her out and moved in with me? Did you know I slept with him after you started dating him?"
"That was then and this is now."
"I will pray for you sweetheart."
"I don't need your prayers, but you need to move on."
"Honey, I am okay today and no longer have to worry about being hit, pushed, or bitten by Mark. Enjoy your life with him."
I hung the phone up.

I prayed for Keke's safety because after two months of knowing Mark, she married him. She did exactly what I did, got caught up in his sex, good food, lies and a glorified painted a picture of himself. I wonder how much time passed before she realized exactly who he is. But that is neither here nor there for me. I'm free.

Mark and I had many conversations after he moved in with Keke in February. I actually missed Mark being in the neighborhood and it took some time for me to really get over him, but I did. I asked myself after he left; what would have happened if Mark never met Keke and stayed down the street from me? Would I have continued to accept his disrespect and abuse? I will never know and isn't interested in knowing. When someone removes themselves out of your life, don't go running after them.

Mark was another lesson in my life because he showed me just how emotionally unstable I still was. He was also a blessing because without that experience, it may have taken me longer to see just how broken I was. I had no respect for myself, men or women. My tongue was very abusive, I was controlling, selfish and very judgmental. More importantly, I lacked self-love. If I loved myself, I would have never allowed anyone to treat me so poorly. I would have never allowed myself to be subjected to such pain and betrayal. There is power in self-love.

Self-love (sĕlf'lŭv')
n. The instinct or desire to promote one's own well-being; regard for or love of one's self.

Every relationship is a lesson and a blessing. We have to walk away willing to find something positive, and move forward to our next destiny. If that destiny is more pain, then you still have much to learn about yourself. Mark didn't happen to me, he happened FOR me. Without Mark, my ugly truth may have not been exposed. Without Mark, I would have never met my beautiful husband. We all have a journey and pain is inevitable. But if we acknowledge our responsibility, learn from our experiences and forgive, we can have the life we desire. It is those who refuse to forgive and those who refuse accountability, and those who refuse to learn from their experiences that live the rest of their lives in misery and chaos. I urge you to self-reflect and recognize exactly what you could have done differently. Thereafter, do the work and I promise your life will begin to have new meaning.

After Mark moved from Blue Island I decided to date myself. I was tired of being mistreated, abused and disrespected by men. I was tired of repeating the same patterns and behaviors I learned from being abused as a child and teen. I decided to do some real time in the mirror and self-reflect. I needed to know why I accepted mistreatment from men; why I lacked self-love and why did I feel like I didn't deserve better. All my answers lied within myself.

Spiritual Journey-10

February 2011

I learned my heart was still full of hate for men. I realized I hadn't forgiven the men who abused Damenia, Chrissy and Nicki. I hadn't forgiven David for his alcoholism and violent behavior. I was still an angry person. That anger blocked me from seeing the things I needed to change. I developed certain patterns and behaviors after being molested and abused and I will spell them out to you.

Falling for Unavailable Men
Confusion about my Sexual Preference
Promiscuity
People Pleaser
Suicidal
Perfectionist
Controlling
Difficulties Saying No to others
Victim Minded
Acceptable to Secrecy
Addictions/Eating Disorders
Engaging in Risky Sexual Behavior
Difficulty Trusting Others
Gossiping
 Always Attracting Chaos/Negativity
Workaholic
Compulsive Liar
Obsessed with Love Relationships
Low Self-Esteem/Self-Worth
Trouble Remembering Abuse

The next questions are how did I conquer all these bad behaviors and patterns? How did I wind up with a beautiful and loving husband? After Mark, I made a conscious decision to stay away from men. I published my first book, Perfectly

Planned and conversed with God as I sat in my car crying. On many days, I found myself talking to God.

"God, I do not want a man. I only want you. I want you to guide me on this new path I am on. I only want you, writing, speaking and helping victims of abuse. Please God help me find my way. I am tired of being used and abused by men and I am tired of being miserable. Please help me. Please help me understand why I continue to accept abuse."

The most important answer I received was to self-reflect and see my ugly truth. I thought I was walking in the light and was walking in darkness. At one point, I suffered from all the patterns and behaviors listed above, but from twenty-eight years old and up to thirty-eight years old, I suffered from these in particular.

Falling for Unavailable Men
Acceptable to Secrecy
Bisexuality
Perfectionist/Controlling
Always Attracting Chaos/Negativity
People Pleaser
Obsessed with Love Relationships
Low Self-Esteem/ Self-Love
Gossiping
Addictions/Eating Disorders

I prayed and read the bible. I searched for the answers that would bring total peace in my life. What I didn't know was writing Perfectly Planned, and reading it released all leftover pain I felt. This wasn't an easy time for me because I isolated myself from most of the outside world. During the day, I spoke at events and during the evening I sat alone with my Bible. I even read Steve Harvey's book, Act Like A Lady, Think Like A Man. I was curious to see what I could learn about men. Once I was able to accept my truth, I was able to channel all of those behaviors and patterns, become a better woman and no longer live wounded.

I finally forgave all the men that abused my family. I forgave David for his alcoholism and all the abuse I saw him inflict on Allen, Chrissy, and Damenia. Lord knows even to this day, I have a true issue with abusive and alcoholic men, but instead of being angry, I pray for them. Once I removed the anger, I looked back on my life and realized what happened to me wasn't my demise. What happened; happened FOR me and not TO me.

I challenged myself and for the first time I rejected any man who approached me if he had a woman. I paid attention to all the signs and asked questions. I learned I subjected myself to chaos and pain so I stood strong, and moved them out of my life. If I really loved myself, I had to understand my value and worth. I had to understand that self-inflicted pain is nowhere near love, and dating another woman's man, leads to a world of pain. I ended that behavior.

I refused to be somebody's side chick, dip or booty call any longer. I refused to be a secret because a man who has me is a blessed man, and is proud to tell the world. According to Steve Harvey's book, Act Like A Lady, Think Like A Man; when a man loves, wants or cares for a woman, he will profess his love and claim her in front of the world. I knew I deserved to be a man's first priority, but I had to do the work. I had to believe in and encourage myself daily.

One of the hardest behaviors or patterns to get rid of was the chaos and negativity. I was born into that type of world. But I understood if I was to move forward and become better, I had to get rid of all the negative people, places and things. I had to remove my stinking, thinking ways. Most of the people I hung with, was because of parties, drinking and eating. Not only that, I had to check the women in my circle. Most of them sought love or had one night stands with men as I did in the past. There was nothing else we had in common. I stopped going to clubs and stopped having parties at my house. I decided to let everybody go. When I looked up, I had no friends at all. I had no choice but to use this as an opportunity to change and better myself. I cried so many days. I felt alone and confused. I had no one; no flesh that it is. It took some time to accept the idea of getting rid of all the people who were in my circle for years, but it was all negativity that I held on to. To make a change, I needed to do it one hundred percent. I needed to surround myself with people who elevated me; people who elevated themselves and people who believed in me. Many days I refused to go out with friends who called me. I didn't want to go out and be around drunken men or women. I had no wish to hang around lusting men in an environment that sin and negativity controlled. The only way I could have a peaceful life was to remove all the negative energy. Negative energy blocks blessings and affirmations works.

Some say being homosexual or lesbian is a choice and others say one is born that way. After being sexually molested by the same sex or forced to engage in sexual activities with the same sex, one will become confused about their sexual orientation. However, that does not make you gay or lesbian. Sleeping with the same sex does not make you gay or lesbian. It makes you a hyper-sexual person. I can not elaborate on what makes a person gay or lesbian, but I can say, being sexually molested by the same sex does not make you gay. I have no desire at all to have sexual relations with a woman.

I learned to stop pleasing others to compensate for my lack of self-esteem. I learned to say no and stand my ground. If saying 'no' caused someone to walk away, then they were not meant for me. I no longer sacrifice myself in an unhealthy way. I no longer agree to do anything I do not want to do in order to please others. I aim to please myself today. Although I have no problem sacrificing myself to help others, I will no longer step on myself.

During my Spiritual Journey, I realized the only love I needed was self-love and with that I no longer sought man's love.

After about three months into my journey, I met Patrick O'Brian Turner and Lord knows I had a weakness for handsome, dark- skinned and well-built men. This is the dialogue I had with God.

"God, I said I did not want any men in my life. Why is Patrick in my life? I only want you. I do not want any men. Lord this man is beautiful with a beautiful heart, but I sense his pain and he will hurt me. I don't want any more pain God; I only want you."

But Patrick never disappeared. He and I became friends, but Patrick suffered from past pain and July twenty-third of 2012, I became Patrick's wife, Mrs. Turner.

Kelley Porter

Self-Reflection-11

Throughout the childhood abuse, toxic relationships with my family, abusive and/or bad relationships with men, I found my purpose and passion. I was blessed with a life full of experiences that many are suffering from today.

Abuse tends to have an everlasting effect on victims and survivors, however once you become an adult; it is time to do the work. The work is self-reflection. You have to look deeply within and be totally honest with yourself about how the childhood abuse affected you. You survived, but is your heart ready and willing to give and receive love.

In order to stand in your truth and live an authentic life you have to accept your ugly truth. If you attract chaos and negativity, you have to accept it. If you don't know what love was, accept it. If you think being slapped in the face or beaten is normal, accept it. If you lack self-esteem and self-love, admit it. If you are insecure, accept it. If you are desperate for a man, accept it. If you are afraid of being alone, accept it. You have to accept these patterns and behaviors because the only way to change is to know what the problem is. What's more, be accountable for your actions.

As adults we make bad decisions and then we blame others. The moment you blame another for wreaking havoc on you, you deny yourself the opportunity to learn and grow. Be accountable for allowing someone to mistreat you. If you are in a domestic violence relationship or just a bad relationship and you have a way out, yet you choose to stay; be accountable. That's not to say you deserve mistreatment or abuse, but it's simply to say you could have made a better decision. We all have choices and when you choose to see your faults, it is then that you begin to grow. Self-reflection leads to self-correction, but the only way to correct, is if you stand in your truth and do the work.

Many of you think you can change a man or woman as I did. Wrong. The only person you need to focus on is yourself. When you focus on changing others you lose your sense of self. It's impossible to see the dysfunctions that live within you. Change can only occur when we accept the fact that there is a problem. How you see and handle any relationship will either stunt or improve your growth. Until you are ready to self-reflect and embrace your ugly truth, I highly suggest, the only person you date is yourself.

Take some time to date and learn self or you will attract another bad relationship. You are what you attract. Dig deep and see exactly what you can do to make yourself better. Otherwise you will take the same person to the next relationship and you will have no one to blame, but yourself. You are not responsible for other's action, but you are responsible for yours. Don't worry about what the last man or woman did, worry about what you did or didn't do. People are who they were before you crossed their paths. Therefore, their actions and behaviors have nothing to do with you and vice versa.

Don't walk away angry. When you walk away angry, you take that same anger to the next relationship and wreak havoc on someone who has nothing to do with your last man or woman. That anger will also block your blessings. How? An angry heart is incapable of seeing, embracing or accepting a blessing; such as a good man or woman. What's more, an angry person lacks faith and love. How can you give someone your whole heart when you are angry? Walk away in peace and know There is something better for you. Wouldn't you rather walk away and suffer for five or ten months than to live the next five or ten years in pain with someone? That's a question.

Being insecure is a sure way to run a man or woman away. Insecurities are unfortunate self-doubts either originating from growing up in a dysfunctional household or being betrayed and deceived as an adult. The unfortunate part is, the behaviors that surface from insecurities, are forced on an innocent person, and can cause unnecessary pain. More than often these behaviors have nothing to do with the other person, but most will try to blame the other person. If you are questioning everything your man or woman does and they haven't given you reason, you are insecure and need to do a self-check.

Lacking self-love is a sure way to end up in a bad or abusive relationship. Why? Because you lack self-love and will accept anything. When you truly love yourself, you will not put yourself in harm's way or allow anyone to mistreat you. Mistakes happen in relationships and sometimes you will get hurt, but you have to know the difference between love and abuse.

I learned a very valuable lesson from my relationship with Grace, Daniel, Mark, Damenia, Chrissy, and Nicki. I learned I was accountable for my actions. Daniel and Mark were who they were before I met them. If I continued to blame them, I wouldn't be able to write this book because I wouldn't be able to add value to your life. I was just as toxic and unstable as Chrissy, Damenia, and Nicki, but I had to admit these things to change them. I had to walk away and really see myself for who I was. I was my demise. The moment you walk away is the moment you have to self-reflect and correct, otherwise get ready for your next toxic, abusive or bad relationship.

In the end you have to make a conscious decision to move forward after being knocked down. It won't happen overnight and isn't easy, but you can do it. Don't look at how hard it is, look forward to meeting the person you will become. Move on with your life and work towards creating a new you. Remove the fear, and break out the buried person.

Trusting After Betrayal- 12

After experiencing sexual abuse, incest, and domestic violence trusting someone, especially a man was very difficult for me. For many years, I kept a shield around me to protect myself. I was so afraid of being hurt, I never allowed anyone to get too close. Sometimes I subconsciously pushed people away because, in my mind, they were going to hurt me or leave me. I was in my way. Today, I no longer have a problem trusting or letting people in my heart. In life someone will always hurt us, however, that pain isn't meant to kill us, it is to strengthen and teach us. The goal is to forgive those who cause you pain and trusting becomes easy.

Any form of abuse, especially as a child will rob you of the way you see the world. The world is not viewed as one who lacks being a victim of sexual abuse or domestic violence. It can take years to define you as well as trust yourself. Trusting others is not the only mission after abuse, trusting yourself and the decisions you make are necessary. As a victim of abuse, you were probably blamed and shamed. Your identity is stolen; your confidence is knocked down and so is the real you. Life is interrupted. This leads to low self-esteem, indecisiveness, lack of self-trust and for others. You may ask yourself how?

As a child, how can you begin to trust yourself if your first encounter with another person was all lies, betrayal and deception? Blaming you, made you doubt yourself. That feeling of "doing something wrong" made you believe you made a bad decision. But, in reality children cannot and are incapable of making a sound decision to have sex. However, your abuser programmed you to believe it was your fault and, since you were a child; manipulation and brainwashing you was easy.

As an adult, you have already developed in your mind how life is, and when you come in contact with, or date an abusive person, your life and beliefs become tainted. As adults, we are very hard on ourselves for making mistakes. But here is the thing, learn from it, accept your responsibility and forgive yourself. Adults are not resistant to mistakes. We error all the time and your errors are experiences that will elevate you, not break you. Don't be ashamed of the mistakes you make or getting involved with someone who wasn't good for you. Don't be embarrassed to seek help. Take those bad experiences and continue to live and walk by faith. Never allow the bad behaviors of someone to change your heart, self and being. They do not deserve that power. Remember an abuser is suffering, and they only have pain to give. Hurt people, hurt people. Pray for them, forgive them, yourself and rise above the pain.

Trust is a very important factor in any relationship. I refuse to allow past deceptions and abuse to stop me from having a successful relationship. You should too. Besides having a successful relationship, when we don't trust we block blessings. Do not isolate yourself out of fear. I urge you to trust the process of life. As long as we live someone will hurt us again, however, don't be afraid of pain; embrace it as your key to the next level of strength.

The most important factor leading to trust others is to forgive. Forgiveness releases the pain, anger and shame and then, you will regain your power. Once you regain your power, the world no longer seems unsafe. It is exactly what it is, a place where everyone makes mistakes, intentional or not. Now you can open yourself up and not worry about being hurt because you have the tools and power to move forward.

Forgiveness-13

I believe to get the strength needed to forgive any source of pain; one will have to do the following.

Grieve - Be Sad/Cry
In most cases when we are hurt by someone we try to suppress the pain. Instead of dealing with it or grieving, we place it deep in our souls hoping it will go away. The problem with that is as long as the pain is present, it will surface and new relationships will be affected. Individuals who have nothing to do with this struggle or pain will feel the wrath from it.

Without grieving, the heart is bitter, and the soul is compromised. By definition I mean, the same pain you felt while being abused or hurt is the same pain that will almost immediately surface. Every new person is compared to the wrongdoer instead of looking at the situation for today. A tarnished heart will always retreat to past pain.

Grieving does not mean going into a depression. It means to have your days of sadness. "Release It" Don't hold on to the pain. *Every tear shed is a sign of strength and freedom to come.* Have your five minutes of self-pity and keep going.

Understanding/Compassion - We all are sinners.
I know it's difficult to have compassion or understanding for anyone who hurts you, so this is the part of forgiveness that makes it so hard toaccomplish. How many times have you hurt someone? We are all human, and we all make mistakes. Whether it was intentional or inadvertent, we all err. How did you feel after you hurt someone and he or she held a grudge against you? Deep in your heart you wanted that person to understand your pain and realize that you needed deliverance as well.

Accept - Accept that the past will never change.
The past can only be accepted and embraced. Accept that you were deeply hurt and left with scars. It will be difficult to move forward, but you can. Life is filled with wrongdoers and as long as you live; you will be hurt again. You have two choices; live or exist. If you choose wisely, life will get better.

Accountability - Be responsible for your own actions.
When an adult stays in a situation that he/she knows is completely toxic, it is their responsibility to realize he or she was just as accountable as the wrongdoer. We have to see our faults, and see what we could have done better. If you know in your heart of hearts that you could have made a better decision, then you are just as accountable as the wrongdoer. Don't place blame on others when you know you could've done better. Placing blame denies you the opportunity to learn. That leads to repeated history. Denial leads to desolation.

Learn From It - Find Something Positive
One of the key elements of forgiveness is to learn from the pain. There is a lesson in everything we experience. It doesn't matter how malicious or callous, there is a lesson and a blessing. To learn from hurt is to gain strength. To learn from hurt is to gain knowledge. To learn from hurt is to grow and mature. Find something positive from your experience. Did you learn something about yourself during this experience? Did it make you a better person? Learn from all experiences, good or bad; they are all blessings.

Have No Fear -14

I lived in, around and beneath fear. My life was covered in fear. I had false expectations that appeared real to me. Why, because I refused to face and overcome my past obstacles and pain. I indulged in a non-reality vision of being happy, and successful, yet I had no faith, plans, goals or visions. My fear of being the best, beautiful, intelligent, confident, secure, authentic, transparent, honest, loyal, happy and successful was all a dream to me because I was covered in fear and not faith. My biggest fear was amounting to nothing after thirty years of uncertainties, toxicity and abuse. I didn't want to face my fears because to me there was nothing in my reality.

I conquered my fears when I shared my life of abuse in my book Perfectly Planned. Since that day, I have changed thousands of lives. Since Perfectly Planned, I have grown confident, courageous, strong, intelligent, secure, transparent, authentic, compassionate, understanding, and somewhat humble. Since Perfectly Planned, I have been blessed with a wonderful husband who loves me with every fiber of his being. Since Perfectly Planned, I have spoken for the educational and the prison system, Non-for-Profit and youth organizations and so much more. Since Perfectly Planned, I have resigned from my staff position as a Medical Technologist (over 23 years in health care) and can now focus on my life's purpose. Since Perfectly Planned, I no longer have fear. Since Perfectly Planned, I have completed my fourth book.

Thought Provoking Questions

1. Are you in an abusive relationship? If so, why are you staying?
2. Did you watch your father physically abuse your mother?
3. Do you understand what Domestic Violence is?
4. Do you love and value yourself?
5. Are you trying to change your spouse/boy/girlfriend?
6. Were you a victim of child molestation?
7. Have you sought within for answers?
8. Were you sexually molested by the same sex? If so, are you gay or lesbian today?
9. Do you blame others for causing you pain?
10. Have you had countless sex partners?
11. Do you know what love is?
12. Did you grow up being abused by your father?
13. Are you afraid to be alone?
14. Does your boyfriend put his mother before you?
15. Do you give more to others than they give to you?
16. Are you willing to be accountable for your own actions?
17. Is the man you're dating involved with someone else? If so, were you aware?
18. Are you allowing people to mistreat you because that's all you know?
19. Did your mother abandon you?
20. Do you believe and have faith in yourself?

ABOUT THE AUTHOR

A successful leader and expert on overcoming all forms of abuse, avoiding toxic relationships and the art of forgiveness, Kelley Porter is a Certified Transformation, and Personal Development Coach, Award Winning Six-time Author, and Professional Speaker. As a speaker, Kelley's transparent and authentic style of speaking will empower anyone to self-reflect, start the process of healing and correct thoughts and behaviors that may hinder them from living a healthy and non-toxic lifestyle.

As a Coach, Kelley empowers you to reach emotional freedom, gain clarity and discover your infinite possibilities. She is well known for assisting in the removal of mental and emotional blocks that hinders people from reaching their fullest potential. Her areas of specialty are, but not limited to; abuse, healing, relationships, thoughts, emotions, and behaviors as she has written books on all topics. Kelley has over thirty years of direct experience with all forms of abuse, domestic violence relationships, creating purpose and power from painful experiences, and creating a positive mindset.

Kelley contributes to society her genuine love for healing, improving awareness and identity, developing talents and potential; enhancing the quality of life and the realization of dreams and aspirations. Kelley's mission is to guide you to design a healthy and meaningful life through wisdom, consciousness, self-reflection, self-love, accountability and forgiveness. Prior to Kelley discovering her life purpose, she spent twenty-three years in healthcare and worked fifteen of those years as a Medical Technologist, as she is a member of the American Society for Clinical Pathologist.

Kelley has been seen and heard on radio and TV including WVON, HOT105 (Florida), Inspiration 1390, WKKC, Channel 2, 5, 7 and 19 and My Black is Beautiful (online). She has been featured in Rolling Out Magazine, Chicago Tribune, Bean Soup Times, SisterSpeak237 (Africa) and spoken for numerous prestigious organizations such as Robert H. McKinney Law School and the Chicago Police Department. She is available for speaking engagements such as keynotes, seminars, workshops, conferences and panels. Her audience can range from congregations, universities, youth groups, NFP and community organizations, the educational and prison system as well as shelters.

Kelley Porter

www.ingramcontent.com/pod-product-compliance
Lightning Source LLC
Chambersburg PA
CBHW052020290426
44112CB00014B/2311